The

COUNTRY LIFE MOVEMENT
IN AMERICA

1900–1920

Kennikat Press
National University Publications
Series in American Studies

General Editor
James P. Shenton
Professor of History, Columbia University

WILLIAM L. BOWERS

The
COUNTRY LIFE MOVEMENT
IN AMERICA
1900–1920

National University Publications
KENNIKAT PRESS • 1974
Port Washington, N.Y. • London

Manufactured in the United States of America

Published by
Kennikat Press Corp.
Port Washington, N. Y./London

Library of Congress Cataloging in Publication Data

Bowers, William L.
    The country life movement in America, 1900-1920.

    (Kennikat Press national university publications,
Series in American studies)
        Bibliography: p.
        1. United States - - Rural conditions. 2. Sociology,
Rural. 3. Agriculture - - Social aspects - - United States.
I. Title.
HN64.B748   301.35′0973   74-80587
ISBN 0-8046-9074-X

To Milly, Dave, Rick, Steve, and Jim

Acknowledgments

Many people have helped me in my work on this study. The late Henry Wallace graciously permitted me to use his grandfather's papers at a time when they were not yet open to researchers. A surprising number of descendants of country life leaders provided me with information, and I am particularly grateful to Mrs. H. Donald Harris, daughter of Charles Moreau Harger, Mrs. Thomas Troxell, daughter of William S. Rossiter, Paul Foght, son of Harold W. Foght, Miss Eleanor M. Sprague, daughter of Robert Sprague, and Will Nelson, son of William Lester Nelson. In my search for personal papers of country life leaders I was aided by archivists across the country, and I wish to thank the following who were particularly helpful: Roy Basler, Library of Congress; Daniel Rylance, formerly archivist at the University of North Dakota; Maynard Brichford, University of Illinois; Miss Barbara Shepherd, Cornell Regional History Collection; J. E. Boell, University of Wisconsin; and, William J. Vollmar, Ohio State University. I am also grateful for the assistance rendered by the library staffs and personnel at the Library of Congress, National Archives, University of Iowa, University of Illinois, Bradley University, and Illinois State University at Normal. Finally, I wish to thank the editors of *Baileya* and *Agricultural History* for their permission to reproduce portions of this study which previously appeared as articles in their journals.

Contents

The

COUNTRY LIFE MOVEMENT

IN AMERICA

1900–1920

Introduction

That a new America of the urban masses was rapidly replacing an older America of the village and farm during the decades near the turn of this century is one of those proverbial facts that all schoolboys know. As early as 1870 the census showed that farmers were a minority among the gainfully employed, and by 1910 less than one-third of the nation's population worked on the land. It is less well known, however, that the accelerating movement of people away from the farms caused widespread and serious concern among early twentieth-century Americans. Although a revolution in transportation, the expansion of industry, and the growing efficiency of agriculture were largely responsible for the noticeable decline of the farm population, many believed that something deficient in rural life was driving people to the cities. They therefore sought to remedy the situation by advancing proposals to increase the attractiveness and efficiency of country living.

This study focuses on the widespread but generally unorganized country life movement to which these people belonged. Ostensibly an effort to promote measures which would make the social, intellectual, and economic aspects of rural life equal to those of urban living, the movement was in reality a complex mixture of rural nostalgia, the desire to make agriculture more efficient and profitable, humanitarianism, and economic self-interest. Its support came chiefly from people in the land

3

grant colleges, the state and federal departments of agriculture, those associated with the rural school and church, and urban groups with either an economic interest in agricultural affairs or altruistic and "social gospel" motivations. The leadership, like that of the broader Progressive movement of which it was a part, was relatively young, comfortably middle class, urban although of rural, Midwestern antecedents, Protestant, and well-educated.

The interest of many of these people in country life reform derived from their belief in the yeoman myth. To such people, farmers represented the best in society, the energetic, intelligent, law-abiding mainstay. Whatever their immediate objectives, the bulk of these reformers hoped to bring about a situation in which the ideals and values of rural society could be preserved in a complex, urbanized world. They did not actually wish to return to a primitive agricultural economy, but they did hope to hold fast to the social and political virtues of the agrarian past while still retaining the material benefits of industrial changes. Living during a transitional period, they sought to have the best for the farmer of both the technological achievements of the twentieth century and the equal and limitless opportunities of the nineteenth century.

But not all country life thinking was sentimental and romantic. Some people in the movement were concerned about scientific management, efficiency, and the systematic use of resources. The lack of direction in much of American development appalled such men and they sought to replace waste and exploitation with scientific control and planning. This, they believed, would guarantee that farmers could continue to provide enough food and raw materials for the nation's growing population despite their decreasing numbers and the end of rich land. Possessing an abiding confidence in the expert who devised solutions after rigorous investigations, these reformers believed they could create an ideal rural civilization by using scientific procedures. Detailed surveys of rural communities were the starting point in this transformation of country life, but it was upon the reformed rural school and extension education that most reliance was eventually placed.

Most of the supporters of the country life movement had an unbounded faith in the efficiency of education, especially agricultural education, which they viewed as the force best able to regenerate rural society. They believed that knowledge would allow men to master the forces of nature and they carried their faith to the point where it parallelled their belief in the spiritual power of rural life to change mankind. Abreast of changes being advocated by progressive educators during the period, reformers demanded that the life of the community be brought into the country school and that learning be through experience and not simply be memorization. They insisted that the rural school supply knowledge that was personal and useful, that would inspire boys and girls with the joy of living in the country, and that demonstrated that intellectual growth, culture, and satisfaction were possible in country life. For those whose formal education was ended, and to treat the immediate problem of agricultural inefficiency, they advocated extension education. In time this agricultural demonstration work became one of the chief devices used by reformers to promote their program of changes, since it seemed to get results and dealt with the ignorance and indifference of men actually on the farm at the time.

In contrast to farm movements of the nineteenth century, which were upwellings of farmer protest against power, the country life movement urged farmers to seek power. This is what "organization" meant to many people in the movement. Much country life rhetoric, like that of the Progressives, seemed to be a complaint on behalf of the unorganized "against the consequences of organization."[1] Organization was a very necessary part of the task of making a farmer a businessman who could compete equally with other economic groups. Some reformers, however, emphasized the social benefits of organization even more than the economic. They insisted that "man lives not by bread alone" and they believed that the goal for farmers should be to live useful and contented lives, not just economically successful ones.

A certain amount of economic self-interest was also present in country life reform efforts. Businessmen who joined the movement wanted to see farmers efficient and prosperous so that they would be satisfied and would stay in the country and continue to be customers. The poorer the land and the farmers, the less machinery and supplies that could be sold. Moreover, if the farmers were more productive, prices would go down for consumers and wages paid to labor would not have to be so high. Also, as farmers failed and went elsewhere, the greater the tax delinquency and the greater the tax burden on city landowners. How much altruism and how much self-interest were involved in some of the efforts carried on by supporters of the country life movement, one cannot know for certain.

These characteristics distinguished country life reform and they reveal something of the ideological basis of the movement, but exactly what groups supported rural reform efforts and why? Who were the leaders and what motivated their actions? How did country life reformers analyze particular aspects of the so-called "rural problem" and what specific proposals did they make to remedy it? What methods did the reformers use to promote their program of change and how did the rural population respond to this concern and activity on their behalf? Finally, how successful was the movement and what accounted for its success or lack of it? This study is an attempt to answer these questions.

chapter one

American Agriculture at the Turn of the Century

The opening years of the twentieth century were a time of transition for American agriculture as they were for society in general. By 1900, expansion in terms of available and easily cultivated lands was rapidly reaching its natural limits, which called for a shift away from extensive to more intensive cultivation. Moreover, important changes which were part of the revolutionary agricultural development and growth set in motion after the Civil War continued to take place.

Technologically, new machines and methods were increasing the capacity to produce with less labor which promised the means for agriculture to keep pace with industrial growth while releasing many of the rural population for urban employment. Although mechanization made its initial impact on agriculture before the Civil War, it was not until afterward that technological change began to affect farming on a large scale and at an accelerated rate. From the end of the war onward, scores of new devices, new crops, new techniques, and even new concepts of farming were offered to farmers, and their increasing use of these innovations brought about remarkable improvements in the efficiency of agriculture.

Economically, a greater amount of capital was required to farm and there was a growing dependence on the market for disposal of agricultural products. The need for capital was especially crucial because the rising cost of farmland and the increasing use of machines and commercial fertilizers demanded greater outlays of funds. Furthermore, the enjoyment of goods such as telephones, household conveniences, stylish clothing, and automobiles which city dwellers were making a part of the American standard of living also required substantial amounts of money. Better credit facilities were therefore demanded by an increasing number of farmers who wanted to see farming become an efficient business.

But as farmers became more commercial, new problems arose for them. Reliance upon distribution agencies and the fortunes of a special crop or type of farming diminished their independence. In a similar way, acceptance of machines created dependence, not alone on the devices themselves, but also on outside supply of so many items of life which were once made on the farm itself. Moreover, farmers were required to be proficient in lines seldom found combined in one individual: strength, endurance, mechanical aptitude, knowledge of scientific agriculture, and financial ability.

Socially, the greater investment needed to farm was making it difficult to shift from hired hand to tenant farmer to owner. In other words, the "tenure ladder" of earlier times seemed to be breaking down. Historically, renting a farm was considered only a step in the progression toward ownership, but with the great increase in land values, many were forced to give up their hopes of ever acquiring a farm of their own. This rise of land prices was largely due, of course, to the closing of the frontier, which decreased the supply of good land available.

Intellectually, traditional rural values were being challenged by scientific knowledge and machine technology. The adoption of the new things of the urban world was followed by the creation of new conventions and dependencies. Specifically, as agriculture was drawn more and more into the orbit of modern business, ideas and morals associated with business extended to the farmers and old practices and ways of living were increasingly abandoned.

Of course, none of these changes took place universally and all at once, but each was a definite part of the observable trend toward the commercialization of farming. On the other hand, a great number of farmers were not involved in this transition at all. Still conducting their enterprises in haphazard fashion and using traditional rule-of-thumb methods, they were eking out a living on the soil. Many seemed only a step away from peasantry.

*　*　*

Probably the most important single development in agriculture during those years was the return of prosperity. In contrast to the closing decades of the nineteenth century, when rural America suffered from economic distress, farmers were making more money and living better than ever before. Admittedly, this situation was not uniform nor equal for farmers across the nation; localities, and even entire regions, did not share fully in the good times. Certainly it is true that conditions in the East and among Southern tenants were different from those in the Middle West and West. But the general circumstances of agriculture appeared more satisfactory than they had been for decades and the period has been subsequently labelled "the golden age of American agriculture." Even now the computation of parity prices is based on the years 1909–1914 when farm receipts and purchasing power came closest to a balance.

"From the beginning of Indiana to the end of Nebraska," declared a farm speaker, "there is nothing but corn, cattle and contentment."[1] Similarly, the author of a book on farming announced that a "new era in agriculture" had raised the annual value of farm products to the "unthinkable sum of six and one-half billions of dollars," which would soon make the farmer's life superior to that of all other Americans.[2] Others made grandiose comparisons to show the dimensions of agriculture's new well-being, as did the writer who asserted that one American harvest would buy Belgium, two would purchase Italy, three, Austria-Hungary, and five, Russia. On a less impressive level, the same writer declared that farmers earned enough in 17 days to buy out Standard Oil and enough in 50 days to "wipe Carnegie and the Steel Trust off the industrial map."[3] Even the *Report of the Country Life Commission* in 1909, while ostensibly a statement of deficiencies in agriculture, affirmed that "there has never been a time when the American farmer was as well-off as he is today, when we consider not only his earning power, but the comforts and advantages he may secure."[4]

The explanation of this marvelous restoration of farm prosperity involves a number of developments which either took place or culminated near the turn of the century. First of all, agricultural expansion slowed down when the frontier "closed" and rich land in large quantities was no longer available. Much of the earlier difficulty faced by farmers was due to the rapid increase in settlement and production which caused supply to exceed demand. Between 1870 and 1890 the number of farms in the United States nearly doubled, and improved acreage enlarged from 188,921,099 to 357,616,755 acres. During the period 1900 to 1920, by contrast, the number of farms increased only from 5,737,372 to 6,488,343, and less than 100,000,000 acres were brought into tillage or used for grazing. Moreover, much of this new land was poor in quality and it did not increase production proportionally.[5]

This slowing down of expansion also brought a stabilization in agricultural output. During the years 1866–1897, wheat production nearly quadrupled, the corn yield more than doubled, and the number of cattle and swine increased about twofold. Between 1897 and 1916, however, wheat production only rose from 530,149,000 to 636,318,000 bushels. The rate of corn production also slackened, although not as sharply, rising from 1,902,968,000 bushels in 1897 to 2,566,927,000 in 1916. Cattle and hog raising showed a similar deceleration after 1897.[6]

Increased demand for farm products due to advancing industrialization and urbanization was another element which brought a return of prosperity to farmers. Industrial growth was a direct stimulant to agricultural well-being during these years through its purchases at good prices of greater and greater amounts of fiber and other raw materials produced by farmers. Indirectly, industry also provided the reason for the increasing demands for foodstuffs since it was responsible for the great urbanization taking place. During the first two decades of the century the city population grew a remarkable 80 percent, which added approximately 24,000,000 more urban consumers.[7] Illustrative of this dramatic growth was the increase of New York City's population from nearly 3,500,000 to over 5,000,000. Similarly, Chicago, the nation's second largest city, increased the number of its residents 58.5 percent during these years. Other American cities recorded even greater gains: Schenectady, New York, 180.7 percent; Youngstown, Ohio, 195.2; Birmingham, Alabama, 306.4; Jacksonville, Florida, 222; Des Moines, Iowa, 103.5; Wichita, Kansas, 192.7; Dallas, Texas, 243.7; Spokane, Washington, 184.2; and Los Angeles, California, 453.1.[8]

The enlarged market created by industrial and urban growth brought farm production more into line with demand, even at a time when agricultural exports were declining. The percentage of American crops going to foreign destinations between 1900 and 1914 actually decreased, although their value rose slightly. For example, the wheat export percentage generally ranged between 25 and 40 percent of the yearly production for the period 1867–1900, but only 10 to 20 percent for the years 1900–1914. Quite obviously, expanded domestic needs were responsible for the increased demand for American agricultural products during these latter years.[9]

A great appreciation of land values after the abundance of cheap, rich land ceased to be available also helped to bring about the revival of farm prosperity. During the first decade of the century, prices for land increased 118.1 percent. In some states, particularly in the Middle West, the advance was even greater. The cost of farmland, for example, rose 123 percent in Iowa, 189 percent in Kansas, 231.8 percent in Nebraska, 321.3 percent in North Dakota, and 377.1 percent in South Dakota. While it is true that mortgage indebtedness was rising at this same time, a great deal of the money borrowed was used for improvements which resulted in raising farm values, providing conveniences, and increasing productivity.[10]

The upturn in other farm prices due to an increase in the gold supply was still another factor which contributed to the renewal of agricultural well-being. Throughout the period between the war with Spain and the First World War the prices farmers received for their products rose steadily, although stabilizing to some extent for the years 1910–1915. If, for comparative purposes, commodity prices for 1899 are viewed as 100, the value of farm production advanced to 106.4 in 1900, to 133 in 1905, to 167.3 in 1908, and 189.2 in 1910. Specific commodity prices followed a similar trend. The price of wheat went from $.73 a bushel in 1896 to $.99 a bushel in 1909, and it remained near that figure until 1915. Corn prices before 1897 generally fluctuated between $.30 and $.45 per bushel, but between 1900 and 1914 corn sold for $.45 to $.70 per bushel. Oats averaged $.32 a bushel for the years 1867–1897, but during the decade after the Spanish-American War they brought an average of $.34 a bushel, and from 1909 to the outbreak of World War I they sold for an average price of $.39 per bushel. Swine prices for the period 1867–1897 generally varied from $4.00 to $5.00 per head, but in 1901 they were up to $6.20 per head, and during the years 1910–1914 they stabilized between $9.00 and $10.00 per head. Cattle prices before 1900 were from $15.00 to $20.00 per head, but between 1909 and 1914 they averaged $20.00 to $30.00 per head. Other farm prices followed a similar contrasting pattern.[11]

Completion of the railroad network with its rapid transportation at relatively reasonable rates, which allowed farmers to specialize in commodities particularly suited to the resources and markets available to them, also aided the restoration of good times to farming. While it is true that farm dissatisfaction with railroad practices continued to manifest itself in the new century, rates were going down and railroad abuses were becoming the objects of effective state and national regulatory legislation. Besides, whether farmers liked them or not, the railroads did play a part in their commercial success.[12]

Finally, farmers were receiving more and more advice on how to increase their profits through better farming and marketing practices. Again, there is the necessary qualification that many farmers still remained hostile to so-called "book farming" and the recommendations of experts whom they considered out of touch with the realities of actual farming. However, progressive commercial farmers, and it was they, after all, who were most prosperous, developed a new respect for these advisers and their stress on the importance of scientific ideas in farming.[13]

The key factor in this explanation of the farmers' new prosperity was the great increase in consumer demand caused by industrialism and the associated urban growth. For without this expanded domestic market which absorbed most of the food and fiber produced by agriculture, farm production would not have attained an equilibrium with consumption. A large part of the farmers' problem in the late nineteenth century was the imbalance between supply and demand caused by unrestrained expansion which resulted in overproduction. Therefore, the leveling off of production at the turn of the century, combined with increased consumer demand, brought agriculture out of the economic doldrums.

*   *   *

Few will dispute that the affairs of agriculture were generally more prosperous during the period under discussion than they had been for several decades. However, an accurate impression of the farm situation must take in more than prosperity and certain other changes. There were also signs that agriculture was declining with respect to the rest of the economy. As the authors of the Country Life Commission's report put it, there were manifestations of an "unequal development of our contemporary civilization."[14] That much of this relative decline was a part of the industrialization of society in no way alters the reality of agriculture's diminishing position.

One indication of the changing importance of agriculture was reflected in its relative loss of people. Although the population of the nation was growing, the percentage which the rural element constituted was decreasing, from 63.9 percent in 1890, to 59.7 percent in 1900, to 53.7 percent in 1910. Even more dramatic was the decrease in the percentage of those actually employed in agriculture during those same years; 42.5 percent in 1890, 37.7 percent in 1900, and 30.7 percent in 1910. From the 1870s, when half of the gainfully employed were in farming, to the 1920s, when the fraction dwindled to less than a quarter, there was a steady contraction of the farm population.[15]

An observable phenomenon associated with this relative population loss was the accelerating migration of country people to the city. A large part of this movement was due, of course, to the increasing efficiency in agriculture, which required fewer people on the land. But apparently some of it was caused by dissatisfaction with poor schools, lack of conveniences and recreational facilities, inadequate roads, isolation, and the alleged general sterility of farm life. The decisive causes, however, were economic and technological.[16]

Whether or not farm people were leaving the countryside because of inadequate facilities, there was accumulating evidence that rural areas were deteriorating in relation to other parts of the nation. Roads were nearly as bad as they had been in pioneer days, schools were poor, health and sanitation measures were meager, household conveniences were lacking, and credit and banking facilities were inadequate. Moreover, there was some truth to the charges that farmers suffered from inequalities of taxation, the tariff, discriminations in transportation, exploitation by middlemen, and the monopolistic control of natural resources.[17]

However, it was the qualification on the farmers' well-being which was most pronounced. Although conditions in agriculture were generally better than they had been, the farmers' gains were moderate when compared to others. Farmers simply were not making as much money as men in other occupations. Perhaps the most convincing testimony concerning this situation was that offered by statistics relative to the filing of the first income tax returns in 1916. At that time everyone with net earnings of $3,000 or more was required to file. Out of approximately six million farmers, 14,407, or one-fourth of one percent, sent in returns. One of every 400 farmers filed compared to one of every 200 teachers, one of every 80 ministers, one of every 22 salesmen, one of every 14 doctors, one of every 9 engineers, and one of every 5 lawyers and bankers. Moreover, 5,984 farmers, or nearly half of those who did submit returns, had earned less than $5,000 net income.[18]

Those concerned about rural development attributed the farmers' lower income when compared to the earnings of many in urban occupations to a number of circumstances. Some pointed out that increases in farm wealth were due to the rise of land prices, but that this was part of the fixed assets in farming and not part of the annual income. There was some basis for this contention since land made up about seventy percent of the value of farm property during the period. The most apparent explanation, however, was the failure of farmers to exchange their produce at fair and profitable prices. With scientific techniques, production was no longer the problem it had once been, but how to make farming pay better through improved marketing practices became one of the burning issues of the day.[19]

To sum up, then, American agriculture at the turn of the century was reaching the limits of natural expansion in terms of easily cultivated lands, and as a result farming and farmers were undergoing changes. Through new methods of agriculture involving technological advances and greater efficiency, farmers made modest gains during these years. Habits, customs, institutions, and ideas of country people were also altered by industrialization and the accompanying urbanization. The role of urban reformers in urging many of these changes on farmers is a major concern of this study, however, and the following chapter surveys urban groups which sought to effect transformations among the country population.

chapter two

The Country Life Movement

To many people living near the turn of the century, the accelerating movement of farmers to the cities was a phenomenon that threatened to destroy the agrarian foundation on which America rested. The rapid decrease of the farm population and the diminished importance of rural society alarmed them because they believed that much that was good in the nation's past was about to be lost forever and they feared for an America dominated by the city. Such people therefore sought to find ways to forestall the possibility.

Convinced that deficiencies in rural living were causing people to move to the cities, they proposed dramatic changes in country life to halt the rural exodus. Some believed that inadequate farm profits were a reason for dissatisfaction and they wanted agricultural practices made more efficient so as to yield a higher return to farming. Others were persuaded that farmers did not receive enough for their produce, and they insisted that something should be done to improve marketing practices, especially as they involved middlemen. A great number of people felt that rural education was not performing its proper function and should be changed to inculcate love of country living and to teach scientific farming methods. The rural church, many asserted, was no longer an active force in promoting satisfaction with farm life. They believed it should be "institutionalized," by which they meant it should be made to teach and practice a social morality and outlook like many urban churches. Some concerned individuals declared that the physical condition of country roads, the subject of growing discussion since the Civil War, were major factors in rural dissatisfaction and would have to be improved. In this way rural isolation would be reduced, farm markets made more accessible, consolidated schools a possibility, and the automobile a practical part of the farmers' standard of living. Still other people stressed that modern commercialized farming required greater outlays of capital and demanded new credit facilities for farmers.

The concern for these changes did not come, as might be expected, from a movement of discontented farmers. Instead, it came primarily from an emerging professional rural leadership and urban elements with either a definite stake in agricultural matters or strong humanitarian, philanthropic, and "social gospel" notions. Among the first to diagnose and offer remedies for country life problems were rural leaders such as the academicians in the land grant colleges, bureaucrats in the Department of Agriculture, men in the new twentieth-century farm organizations, and editors and publishers of prominent farm journals. Bankers, retail merchants, farm implement manufacturers, mail-order houses, railroads, transportation companies, chambers of commerce, and boards of trade were some of the urban groups which recognized the connection between their prosperity and the farmers' and therefore took an active interest in rural welfare. Teachers, ministers, social workers, charitable institutions, and civic betterment leagues were representative of groups which joined the movement from more altruistic motives.[1]

State agricultural colleges and the experiment stations affiliated with them were in the forefront of the effort to help farmers adjust to changing conditions and increasing pressures. Through numerous bulletins, short courses, and a variety of extension programs, they encouraged agriculturalists to use new and tested ways of farming. Although the major emphasis was on improved methods of production, a few forward-looking academicians were developing courses in farm management, agricultural economics, and rural sociology. These new fields received little notice at the time, but they were destined to become important to twentieth-century American agriculture. Moreover, some of the men who pioneered them became influential in the movement to improve country life by ameliorating rural social conditions.

The United States Department of Agriculture was also conducting research and transmitting useful knowledge to farmers through bulletins and circulars. In many ways, its work in applying the principals of science to agricultural production parallelled that of the land grant colleges. During the period, however, the department did accept a new function when it sponsored the educational demonstration work which was nationalized by the Smith-Lever Act. Still, the leading policy of the federal department, like that of the agricultural colleges, was to make two blades of grass grow where only one grew formerly. This was adhered to even in the face of mounting evidence that the real source of the farmers' disadvantageous economic position was the inequity of the marketing system and the resulting maldistribution of profits. Both the federal government and the state colleges of agriculture gave little attention to the marketing situation until farmers themselves set up their own cooperative associations and began exerting political pressure in their states.[2]

When David F. Houston became Secretary of Agriculture in 1913, the Department finally responded to demands that it undertake work of a social and economic nature rather than limiting its concern exclusively to problems of production. Among its new activities was an inquiry into the needs of farm women and the establishment of what was to become the Bureau of Home Economics. Under Houston's direction, the department also created the Rural Organization Service, which studied farming communities and distributed information on local community organization. Moreover, farm tenancy and marketing received attention for the first time, although interest in the latter came in the wake of farmer agitation, which culminated in the establishment of the Office of Markets.[3]

At the state government level, boards or commissions of agriculture were formed to aid farmers in a variety of ways. Some of these helped farmers to organize and lobby at the state capital for special farm legislation, while others promoted fairs and disseminated information through circulars and bulletins. In New England, where there were a considerable number of abandoned farms, state boards of agriculture printed catalogues which described farms no longer being tilled and attempted to get people to return to the land.[4]

Business interests which supported country life efforts were especially drawn to financing and promoting demonstration education among farmers. This interest began in 1903, when the merchants and bankers of Terrell, Texas, backed the work of Seaman A. Knapp, the leading proponent of demonstration work at the time, in his campaign against the boll weevil. In 1906, the General Education Board, through which John D. Rockefeller carried on some of his philanthropic activities, began contributing money to the effort. A dramatic financial contribution came in 1912, when the President of Sears, Roebuck and Company, Julius Rosenwald, offered $1,000 to each of the first hundred counties in the nation to hire a farm adviser. In fact, after 1909, a major concern of business groups was the passage of a federal law which would nationalize the county agent system of agricultural demonstration work. The businesses and associations involved are too numerous to list completely, but some of the more prominent ones were the American Bankers' Association, the National Implement and Vehicle Association, John Deere and Company, International Harvester Company, Universal Portland Cement, Company, American Steel and Wire Company, Wells Fargo and Company, the National Association of Retail Merchants, the Council of North American Grain Exchanges, the National Soil Fertility League, the Western Lumberman's Association, the Southern Lumberman's Association, the Great Northern Railroad, the Pennsylvania Railroad, and the Rock Island, Nashville, Chattanooga and St. Louis Railroad.[5]

A related activity was that of the railroads, which ran "farm trains" displaying educational exhibits and presenting demonstrations through rural districts. There were, for example, corn and oat specials in Iowa and South Dakota, "good roads" trains in Illinois and Missouri, a "rice train" in Arkansas, a "cotton train" in Louisiana, a dry-farming special in Texas, horse and wheat trains in Kansas, and a dairy special in Wisconsin. Since the chief emphasis on these trips was the promotion of more production, railroads were eager to operate such trains, for they were paying propositions in that the more the farmers produced, the more freight there would be to carry.[6]

Individual railroads had their own peculiar projects to promote agricultural uplift. The Southern Railway Company, for example, supported the good roads movement, hired agents to advise farmers in the South, and encouraged diversification of Southern agriculture. The Wabash gave a $50 scholarship to the agricultural college for each of the counties in a state through which its line passed. The Great Northern promoted experimental plots along its lines to encourage the use of scientific methods. Owners were paid for using the new methods and were allowed to keep the crop in addition. Still other railroads sold improved seed varieties at cost.[7]

Railroad magnate James J. Hill of the Great Northern was one of the more ardent businessmen who advocated scientific agriculture as an aspect of the conservation of resources. Convinced that the food supply would soon be inadequate if farmers persisted in their wasteful practices, he worked tirelessly during the closing years of his life to improve agricultural methods and the quality of livestock. At every opportunity he expressed his views from the platform and in 1910 published them in a book entitled *Highways of Progress*. Impatient with the information-disseminating programs of the land grant colleges and the Department of Agriculture, he established the five-acre experimental plots along his railroad lines and aided in the adoption of the county agent system in the Pacific Northwest as a more rapid means to the goal of an improved agriculture.[8]

Bankers supported the extension system idea, but also worked to secure other aids to farmers, especially agricultural education in high schools. It was the opinion of many bankers that the inadequate education farm youth received drove them to the city; therefore, bankers campaigned to get legislation passed in the states which would encourage and partially subsidize vocational agriculture courses in the public schools. In Minnesota, which was one of the first states to have such a program, any school adding a vocational education course to its curriculum received $2,500 per year from the state.[9]

Like the railroads, bankers' associations in the various states had individual projects. The Minnesota Bankers Association sponsored corn-growing contests and awarded more than $800 per year in prize money starting in 1913. In 1911, North Dakota bankers in conjunction with a group of Minneapolis businessmen established the Better Farming Association of North Dakota, which hired agricultural experts to work with farmers to increase production. Wisconsin bankers worked to secure better seeds for farmers, while New York bankers urged farmers to try systems of accounting and credits used by merchants. Illinois bankers were instrumental in getting an appropriation through Congress as early as 1909 to extend the Knapp system of demonstration farming to Northern states. Bankers in over a dozen states worked with the state library to bring information to farmers—in most instances, local banks actually established a lending library in the bank itself. In the end, bankers everywhere hoped their efforts to promote scientific practices through education would make farming more attractive and efficient.[10]

Sears, Roebuck and Company, a mail-order house at the time, established an Agricultural Foundation, which supplied farmers with simple information on marketing, farm economics, and production. The firm also organized national seed corn and single-stalk cotton shows with prizes offered for the best specimens. Buoyed up by the general prosperity and parcel post legislation of the years after 1897, Sears, Roebuck recognized the link between its fortunes and the farmers' and it acted accordingly.[11]

In 1909, John D. Rockefeller gave one million dollars to establish the Rockefeller Sanitary Commission for the Eradication of Hookworm Disease. This action came as a result of the impressive work of Dr. Charles Wardell Stiles, attaché to the Country Life Commission in 1908, who demonstrated that hookworm was the hitherto undiagnosed disease common to rural areas of the South. Stiles showed that the parasite causing the disease, which out of ignorance was called the "germ of laziness" by many, was susceptible to a simple treatment with thymal and salt costing less than fifty cents.[12]

Rockefeller moneys were also used to improve rural education and to promote research to determine the causes of the decline of the country church. Moreover, when the Department of Agriculture created the Office of Rural Social Organization in 1913, the Rockefeller organization agreed to work cooperatively with the new division. One of the more ambitious programs which the largess of the Standard Oil magnate proposed to underwrite, however, was the attempt to build up a model agricultural county in Mississippi. Equipped with an agricultural college as a social center, the county was to serve as inspiration and example to those who worked for efficiency and social planning in rural affairs.[13]

Perhaps one of the most outstanding accomplishments of the period for farming was the plan for world-wide agricultural cooperation conceived and brought to fruition by David Lubin, a California businessman. Convinced that crop information ought to be made available to all, not just to the great buyers of the world, Lubin set about to get the nations of both hemispheres to cooperate in a system of crop-data gathering and dispensing. Like a twentieth-century Columbus, he went from country to country in Europe and America attempting to get one of them to lead in the effort. He failed until he came to Italy, where he befriended Guglielmo Ferrero, the Italian philosopher of history, who used his influence with King Victor Emmanuel. The king not only supported Lubin's work, but also gave a palace in Rome, Villa Umberto, for the organization's headquarters. Called the International Institute of Agriculture, the agency became a kind of "World Department of Agriculture."[14]

Urban social reform organizations originally created to remedy city problems also joined the movement to ameliorate rural conditions. For example, the American League for Civic Improvement, which was formed in 1900 to uplift urban life, maintained in 1902 that the country needed improving as much as or more than the city. As a result, it launched a broad program for enhancement of the country environment, including the building of bicycle and foot paths, beautification of country homes and highways, and the placement of restrooms, parks, and playgrounds in rural villages and market towns. In a similar way, the National Conference of Social Work and some state conferences began to devote attention to rural advancement and related topics.[15]

Women's clubs, which had been formed as cultural organizations for urban women and later transformed into urban civic service groups, also became interested in the rural situation. Their activity on behalf of rural life centered about rural school betterment, the uplifting of farm women, and health and sanitation matters, but they were especially diligent in their work to improve the teaching and physical facilities of rural schools. A related project was their support of efforts to have home economics introduced into the curriculum. In addition, they worked with local health and sanitation agencies, and even cooperated with the

Rockefeller Sanitary Commission in its program of hookworm eradication in the South. Another activity sometimes undertaken by these women's organizations was providing rest rooms for farm women and children to use when they came to the city.[16]

On the community level, aroused individuals formed village improvement societies, "people's clubs," and "rural progress leagues" to improve their rural communities. Although such groups used a variety of schemes to encourage improvement, their major objectives were generally those of physical beautification, more adequate facilities for social life, and better roads, schools, and churches. To coordinate their efforts, some of these organizations joined together in federations which included all the groups and agencies interested in country life in a given area. Prominent among such associations were the "Hesperia movement" in Hesperia, Michigan, the Rhode Island League for Rural Progress, the New England Conference for Rural Life Progress, the Illinois Federation for Country Life Progress, and the Pennsylvania Rural Progress Association.[17]

One of the most active and effective agencies working for country church improvement was the Department of Church and Country Life of the Presbyterian Board of Home Missions, which was organized in 1909. Under the leadership of Warren H. Wilson, a minister with training in sociology, it made a series of sociological surveys, printed leaflets and pamphlets, held country church conferences, and worked vigorously to prepare ministers for rural church service. By 1912, the Methodists inaugurated a similar program, as did other Protestant denominations before the period ended [18]

The Federal Council of Churches of Christ in America was another church organization active in the country life movement. As its name suggested, it was primarily concerned with federating churches, but during the years near the turn of the century it was also interested in extending the social role of country churches. With its encouragement, area and state federations combining various denominations and sects were formed to consider the special problems of the rural church. Among these unions were the New England Country Church Association and state federations in Massachusetts, Wisconsin, and Nebraska. In addition, denominational committees for rural church progress existed in at least another dozen states scattered across the nation.[19]

Country Young Men's Christian Association workers were also involved in country life uplift, concerning themselves with the physical, social, educational, and religious welfare of rural people. Like other organizations which supported rural reform efforts, country "Y's" made sociological surveys, worked with agricultural experts, and presented practical talks and demonstrations concerned with various aspects of country life. However, they also attempted to break down some of the isolation of farm life by acting as social centers and even published a small monthly magazine, *Rural Manhood,* devoted to farm and country life matters.[20]

Educational organizations and institutions were, as one might expect, in the forefront of efforts to redirect the rural school during the early years of the century. As early as 1906, when the National Society for the Promotion of Industrial Education was formed to press for a federal vocational education bill as the culmination of years of agitation, country life supporters were included and soon made instruction in agriculture an objective as well as mechanical training. Two years later the National Education Association, which represented many public school teachers and administrators, created a Department of Rural and Agricultural Education within its organization, and from that time on included a consideration of rural schools and agricultural education in its program. This action came somewhat tardily in view of the revelation of educational deficiencies by the Committee of Twelve on Rural Schools a decade earlier. In a similar way, some state teachers associations and numerous educational conferences began to express their awareness of the rural educational system and made proposals to improve it.[21]

During these same years, land grant colleges, normal schools, and governmental agencies also began to concern themselves with agricultural training in the rural public schools and in the preparation of country schoolteachers. As a result, agricultural colleges and normal schools began to offer courses in rural sociology and agricultural economics and to expand extension programs already in existence. About this same time the Office of Experiment Stations of the United States Department of Agriculture and the Bureau of Education of the Department of the Interior indicated their interest in agricultural training by adding rural education experts to their staffs. In 1911, the latter agency also established

a Division of Rural Education, which became an important dis-
seminator of information concerning school surveys, the training
of rural teachers, and all other phases of country school progress.[22]

These activities of educational and religious organizations
directed toward changing the rural church and school were among
the most prominent aspects of the country life movement. In part
this was because such institutions were present in all rural communities and their reformation and concomitant leadership promised a means to the amelioration of other rural problems. Moreover, country life efforts aimed at institutionalizing the rural
church and reorienting the country school to its environment can
be seen as the rural equivalents of the broader "social gospel" and
progressive education movements.[23]

Some farmers, generally the more wealthy, businesslike, and
progressive in their thinking, also joined the country life movement. Reacting to the increasing commercialization of agriculture
near the turn of the century, they began to establish dairymen's
associations, truck gardening exchanges, and similar organizations to disseminate information about production and marketing procedures. Despite earlier failures of cooperative efforts
among farmers, there was revival of interest in cooperation, and
marketing associations geared to performing the functions of
middlemen soon sprang up across the nation. Furthermore, two
new farm organizations were founded during the period, the
Farmers' Educational and Cooperative Union and the Society of
Equity, and they, too, made improved collective marketing practices their chief objective.[24]

But not all farmers who joined the movement were concerned primarily with the economic aspects of agricultural improvement. Some took an increasing interest in clubs, recreational
facilities, and other social and cultural activities. It was probably
no coincidence that the Grange, which from its beginning stressed
the social aspects of country life, also experienced a resurgence
during the period.

*   *   *

The great galvanizing event in the history of the rural reform
movement of the early twentieth century was the appointment of
the Commission on Country Life by Theodore Roosevelt in 1908.
The publicity given its investigation stirred greater interest in
rural problems and its report, which summarized deficiencies and

recommended methods of improvement, was subsequently used as an authority by reformers. Moreover, the commission's emphasis on the use of the survey also gave the movement a concept of reform based on scientific appraisal and planning which became one of its hallmarks.[25]

The investigative body which Roosevelt named during the closing months of his administration was an impressive group of academicians, journalists, public servants, and practical organizers. Liberty Hyde Bailey, the chairman, and Kenyon L. Butterfield were educators in the land grant colleges. Bailey was dean of the New York College of Agriculture at Cornell University and an internationally-known horticulturist, while Butterfield was president of the Massachusetts State College of Agriculture and a rural sociologist. Gifford Pinchot, who had much to do with influencing the President to appoint the commission, was a member of a prominent Eastern family, the chief forester in the Department of Agriculture, and an ardent conservationist. Walter Hines Page of North Carolina edited *World's Work* magazine, a progressive journal of the period, and was an authority on education, sanitary conditions, and farming in the South. Henry Wallace, an Iowan affectionately called "Uncle Henry" by his admirers, was editor of *Wallaces' Farmer* and an influential agricultural spokesman in the Midwest. Charles S. Barrett of Georgia was president of the Farmers' Cooperative and Educational Union of America, a rising twentieth-century farm organization with its main strength in the South at the time. He was added to the Commission when the *Southern Ruralist* of Atlanta demanded that another Southerner be appointed. Californian William A. Beard, editor of the *Great West Magazine* and chairman of both the Sacramento Valley Improvement Association and the National Irrigation Society, joined the commission at the same time to forestall possible protest from the Far West.[26]

The commission was called together in August, 1908, and charged with reporting upon existing social, economic, and education conditions in the country, the means available for remedying deficiencies, and the best methods to use to organize a permanent investigation. Since a report was to be made by January 1, 1909, there was not enough time for a detailed scientific survey. The commissioners therefore used four methods to gather information. First, they sent out a list of twelve questions to some

550,000 country residents whose names were furnished by the
Department of Agriculture and other rural agencies. By the time
the report was presented to the President, they had received about
115,000 responses and the Census Bureau had classified and tabulated almost 100,000 of these. As a second procedure, they gathered information by personal correspondence and inquiries. For
example, Butterfield conducted research into the country church
problem and Wallace inquired into the farm labor-tenancy situation. Next, they toured twenty-nine states, where they held hearings at thirty places. The commissioners stated in their report
that the majority of people attending these meetings were country
folk, but this is not to be construed to mean that they were farmers
for an examination of the minutes shows that most of those who
spoke were nonfarmers. Finally, they encouraged country people
to hold meetings in local school buildings to discuss rural problems and to forward the results to the commission. Apparently
thousands of these meetings were held and in some states specific
days were designated for simultaneous meetings in all country
schoolhouses.[27]

The purpose, methods, and personnel of the commission
caused considerable discussion among the American public in
general. As Clayton Ellsworth has pointed out, newspapers and
magazines gave the commission about as much space as a barn-
storming big league baseball team would have received in that
era. The *Literary Digest* concluded that most of this press comment was sympathetic to the project, but evidence indicates that
there were varying degrees of approval and considerable opposition.[28]

Those who favored the work of the commission emphasized
that it was a long overdue recognition of the farmers' problems,
and they urged cooperation with the investigators. Others praised
Roosevelt for his action and compared its importance to the
"square deal" and the conservation movement. Some agreed
that rural problems needed attention but questioned the effectiveness of such a hasty inquiry.[29]

On the other hand, critics of the commission frequently
charged that it was an election trick to win farm support in the
forthcoming election and that it was unconstitutional paternalism. Many thought, too, that the investigation was unnecessary
since farmers were generaly prosperous and could solve whatever

problems they had by themselves. Others resented what they termed the commission's "slumming" in the poorer rural regions, asserting that the urban indigent needed more help than farmers. A good many wondered why this particular investigation would be successful in finding answers to such problems as how to keep boys on the farm and where to find a source of agricultural labor when theorizers had been searching for years for answers and had not yet found them. Still others dismissed the commission as ineffectual and stressed the need for the federal government to do something about the tariff and similar discriminations against the farmers.[30]

But in spite of the criticism of the commission, many reformers enthusiastically supported the idea of an investigation of American rural institutions by a body of experts. In an examination of farm life conditions such as the one undertaken by the commissioners they saw the promise of an experiment in the revitalization of rural society by means of scientific planning and techniques. The work of the commission, therefore, was to them the very essence of country life progress.

Despite hard work and good intentions, the commission was not able to submit its final report to the President until the end of January, 1909. In it the commissioners made three broad recommendations. One, they urged a redirected education for rural residents through a nationalized extension service which would emanate from the agricultural colleges and utilize lectures, correspondence courses, and demonstration work. Two, they suggested a scientific stock-taking of the country life situation by means of a series of agricultural surveys conducted throughout the nation. Three, they asked that Congress establish some central agency to guide a campaign for rural progress.[31]

Roosevelt was pleased with the report and sent it to Congress for consideration. The Congressmen, who were perturbed by the President's appointment of the commission without their approval, not only refused his request for $25,000 to print and circulate the findings but also ordered the group to stop its activities. Subsequently, the lack of congressional response was matched by the failure of executive interest under Taft, and the life and work of the commission came to an end.[32]

* * *

The country life movement was not so much a "group on

the march," then, as it was a set of impulses, each of which was distinct yet bound to the others by the common desire to do something about the existing status of rural life. However, a discernible difference in viewpoint with respect to the nature of the agricultural pursuit resulted in contrary emphases and separated participants into major categories.

On the one hand were those who viewed farming as a business enterprise which should be operated efficiently and profitably. Prominent upholders of this position were urban businessmen, leaders of the new farm organizations, and some farmers who supported country life efforts. Their prescription for farm life improvement consisted mainly of urging farmers to use scientific practices, increase their capitalization, seek additional governmental aid, and organize for their economic benefit. Any social problems farmers might have, they believed, would be solved when their income was increased.

In the other category were those who looked upon farming as a way of life and farmers as superior beings because of their lives spent close to the land and nature. Largely academicians from the land grant colleges, people associated with the rural school and church, and urban social workers, they emphasized the need for the social development of farm life. To these people there were factors which transcended economic and technical concerns, and they were convinced that the farm population's ultimate salvation lay in moral and social uplift rather than material prosperity.

This fundamental dichotomy in country life attitudes manifested itself in a curious mixture of rhetoric affirming the agrarian myth and practical advice on how to farm. But more importantly, it led to confusion and conflict when attempting to formulate a viable ideology for the movement. For while some groups stressed making farmers into businessmen, the nostalgic attachment of the others to days when farmers enjoyed a higher, more secure status resulted in a contrary preachment that farming was not a business but a way of life. Some reformers tried to reconcile the viewpoints by asserting that modern farming was both a business and a way of life. However, this was not true, for what was needed to make farmers into businessmen was necessarily destructive of the fundamental values of the traditional agrarian way of life. The most obvious proof of this is the fact that farmers cannot be urged to organize and still maintain their age-old individualism. Furthermore, one could not ask the government to intercede on the farmers' behalf or aid them without the independent and self-help image of agrarians being violated. Nor could one urge farmers to imitate urban business counterparts without doing something drastic to the unique aspects of rural living. Regrettably for those who would have the best of both worlds, the urbanization of farmers destroyed the rural way of life.

During the early years of the new century the groups tried to harmonize their objectives despite the serious duality. The journals and meetings of those who saw agriculture as a business gave consideration to conditions of country living, and the surveys, conferences, and periodicals of those who viewed farming as a way of life included information, discussions, and articles on commercial aspects of agriculture. But in 1919 the elements in the country life movement parted. Those who emphasized the idea that farming was a way of life founded the National Country Life Association in that year, while at the same time those whose chief concern was agricultural economics began organizing the American Farm Bureau Federation, which was officially established in the following year.

chapter three

Reformers: Men and Motives

The people in the country life movement were apparently not farmers for the most part. As already noted, groups supporting the efforts to improve rural life included altruistic social workers, land grant college personnel, and businessmen. Governmental agencies and persons identified with the rural school and church were also involved. But what else characterized the country life reformers and why were they so concerned about the conditions of agriculture and farm life?

In an effort to answer these questions, the writer collected and analyzed biographical data for a representative sample of the country life leadership. Since there is no roster of reformers for the period, certain criteria and some subjective judgments had to be used to draw up a list of the most active, articulate, and dedicated people. Prominence in country life conference programs, service on farm commissions, authorship of books and articles on rural life subjects, and agricultural survey or research work were used as evidence of membership in the movement. In some instances, letters and statements of others supplemented these primary standards. Originally, a list of about 150 persons was compiled, but this was ultimately trimmed to eighty-four names when some were removed because they seemed to have only incidental interest in rural reform, or because information about them could not be found.[1]

Almost ninety percent of these leaders were from the farms

and small towns of the nation, but since the population was mostly rural during the last century when these men were born, their rural backgrounds were not unusual.[2] Thirty-eight, or nearly half of them, were born or reared in the Midwest. Only three persons in the sample were born in large cities, two in New York and one in Baltimore. Eight of the leaders were born abroad, but one was born of American parents and three others were born in Canada. Country life reformers then, seemed to have rural antecedents in most instances and Midwestern origins in many cases.

An examination of the educational background of the reformers suggests they were intellectuals. Among the group studied there were seventy bachelor's degrees, forty master's, twenty-two doctors of philosophy, two doctors of medicine, and one doctor of science.[3] Sixteen of the leaders studied in Europe, generally in German universities, and three earned degrees there. In addition, eleven attended college but apparently received no degrees. Four others were privately educated. In the entire group, only four had merely public school educations, and even then two of those studied law and were admitted to the bar.

A statistical study of the places where these degrees were earned showed that sixty-eight colleges, universities, and seminaries were represented. However, twenty-six of the 135 degrees, or about twenty percent, came from Harvard, Michigan Agricultural College, Columbia, and the University of Chicago. There appears to be a relationship between the expertise of some of the people in the movement and the training they received at the latter three institutions. Michigan Agricultural College was the first state institution of higher learning established to train agriculturists and it maintained a leadership among agricultural schools into the twentieth century. The association of John Dewey with Columbia Teachers College and the progressive thought in education which emanated from that institution is sufficiently well-known to require no comment. Likewise, the University of Chicago was earning a reputation during the years near the turn of the century for its sociology courses.[4]

Occupationally, most country life reformers were either educators or journalists. In the sample, forty persons were identified as teachers, while data on several others indicated that they taught in colleges or the public schools either before or

after the period.[5] Twenty-one people in the sample were journalists, two-thirds of them editors. About half of these editors
ran farm journals. The rest of the people were scattered
among various occupations, including businessmen, directors of
philanthropic foundations, clergymen, experts in the Department of Agriculture, and farm organization leaders. Two in-
herited their wealth.[6]

Analysis of the teaching specialties of the educators showed
a preponderance of agricultural and professional education subjects. Of the forty academicians, nine taught scientific agriculture, eight taught rural economics and economics, nine taught
rural sociology or sociology, and fourteen either taught education courses at the college level or taught and administered in
the public schools. Altogether, the agricultural-educational influence directly touched fifty-seven percent of those included in
the sample, either by their training in agricultural colleges or
normal schools or by their work as teachers in such institutions.
Indirectly, of course, it touched nearly everyone in the movement. It should also be noted that the prominence of rural
economists and sociologists was both cause and effect of the
country life movement. For, as interest in the peculiar economic
and social aspects of farming created these new disciplines, the
men who pioneered them became leaders in the effort to bring
about rural life changes.

Further evidence of the interest rural life reformers had in
the new social sciences and scientific efficiency is found in the
organizations to which they belonged and the nature of their
writings. Nearly forty percent of those in the sample were members of either the American Association for the Advancement
of Science, the American Sociological Society, the American
Economic Association, the Society for the Promotion of Agricultural Science, or the American Association of Agricultural
Engineers. Moreover, a great number of the books and articles
written by country life leaders were concerned with increasing
agricultural and educational efficiency.[7]

Likewise, the affinity between country life and conservation policies and activities is shown, to some extent, by the number involved in both movements. Although the indication of
dual participation could be found for only fourteen percent of
the total sample, nearly fifty percent of a group of twenty-six

of the most active leaders were both conservationists and rural uplifters.

By now it is apparent that the leadership of the country life movement was extremely well-educated, generally with rural, Midwestern backgrounds, and interested in the social sciences, education, and scientific agriculture and efficiency. But additionally, rural reformers seemed to be cut from the same cloth that produced Progressive reformers in general. A comparison of the present analysis of the country life group with George Mowry's findings concerning the men and women in the Progressive movement at large seems to confirm this.[8] Like Mowry's group of reformers, those who worked for the amelioration of country life conditions were relatively young. Most of them were born between 1855 and 1875 and their median age was forty-three in 1909 when the release of the Country Life Commission's report signaled the flowering of country life reform.[9]

There is also evidence that these men and women, like Mowry's Progressives, came from comfortable, economically secure stations in life, for almost all of them had college educations at a time when such an education signified membership in a special economic group. Moreover, many of these people received their training in the late nineteenth century, when agricultural depression was widespread, suggesting that their parents, if farmers, were not the downtrodden types identified with the agrarian revolt of that period. In the few instances where parents' occupations were found, there were, in addition to farmers, judges, doctors, ministers, and college presidents.

Religious affiliation was difficult to find, but where given, it supported Mowry's contention that reformers were predominantly Congregationalists and Presbyterians. However, among country life reformers, there were many Methodists and Baptists as well. The prevalence of these evangelistic associations offers a possible explanation for the moralistic flavor and missionary zeal which characterized so much country life activity. Being a good citizen, one reformer stated, "implies the *use* of the Ten Commandments and the primary principles enunciated by Jesus Christ in the affairs of everyday life." To people with such a religious attitude, rural areas could be viewed as needing salvation and those who labored to uplift them as doing the Lord's will.[10]

Political affiliation was even more difficult to identify. In the end, it was obtained for a little more than half of the sample. Even then there was no indication as to how these men aligned themselves in the late nineteenth century, when farmer agitation and silver mania convulsed the country. Nonetheless, of the forty-five for whom affiliations were found, twenty-four were Republicans, sixteen were Democrats, three called themselves "Progressives," one, an "Independent," and one, a Socialist. Possibly it is these latter three designations, plus the fact that four Republicans identified themselves as "Progressive Republicans," which is important, for these suggest that there was some liberal political ferment among country life reformers. On the other hand, perhaps it is most significant that so many failed to give their political affiliations in their biographical materials since it suggests the possibility that these men were not really very interested in politics, not interested enough to identify strongly with any political party.[11]

                              *   *   *

It seems clear from the foregoing analysis that the leaders of the country life movement were generally nonfarmers and urbanites. Furthermore, they were well-educated, economically secure, middle class people who seemingly had little in common with agriculturists. It should therefore be enlightening to consider what it was that motivated them to be interested in the plight of farmers.[12]

For a great many of these reformers, interest in country life matters came largely from their concern with the diminishing position of agriculture, symbolized by such things as a decreasing population, abandoned farms, and a smaller contribution to the national income. Nostalgia for a way of life that seemed to be in eclipse characterized much of the writing of these reformers. Living at a time when the agrarian tradition was still very strong, their anxiety is therefore understandable in terms of their fear that the farmers' position, largely taken for granted, was going by default unless something drastic were done.

Such people recalled with satisfaction that the United States was established as a nation of farmers and they affirmed with pride that its most cherished values and institutions were uniquely shaped by rustic antecedents. Like many in other generations, however, their attachment to farmers and rural living was romantically sentimental and based on certain fanciful ideas about country people and farm life. Central among their beliefs was the concept of landowning American farmers as superior people. According to this viewpoint, the farmers' individualism and independence made them morally upright, simple, and contented, while their close association with nature caused them to be more healthy, virtuous, and religious than others. Their assumed physical strength and courage, moreover, made them a bulwark of military prowess in times of national crisis. A concomitant idea held that agriculture was the fundamental employment of man upon which all other economic activities were vitally dependent.[13]

Neither the "agrarian myth," as this complex of beliefs about the farmer has been called, nor "agricultural fundamentalism," the label given the insistence upon the primacy of farming, were new ideas at the turn of the century. On the contrary, they were formulated originally by writers of antiquity and have been repeated continuously down through the centuries. Hesiod, Virgil, and other ancient writers praised the rustic virtues of country life with essentially the same rhetorical clichés as those used by people at the beginning of the twentieth century and by farm spokesmen of the present. Similarly, the ancient comparison of agriculture to the roots of a tree has its modern counterpart. For example, the late Bernard Baruch called farms the roots of the tree of national life and stated that "we all flourish or decline with the farmer."[14] In American history it was, of course, Thomas Jefferson who was most identified with agrarian idealism and the concern for the small landholding class.[15]

Just as farm life ennobled men, city life supposedly subverted them. Urbanites, it was believed, had wandered from direct contact with the land and were therefore subservient to all the corrupting influences of the city, which was thought to be an alluring but evil place. To people who held such antiurban attitudes, city life was an ugly, competitive struggle for money, whereas farming was a wholesome, satisfying way of life.

"The city sits like a parasite, running out its roots into the open country and draining it of its substance," Liberty Hyde Bailey asserted. "The city," he continued, "takes everything to itself—materials, money, men—and gives back only what it does not want."[16] Moreover, reformers believed that cities needed the "fresh blood" of the country "to repair the physical, mental and moral waste." Some country life leaders even wondered whether the nation could survive if the tendency toward urbanization continued, for eventually there would be no people in the country to revitalize the cities.[17]

The rural antecedents of many country life leaders undoubtedly account for some of this rural nostalgia and antiurbanism. It seems probable, however, that not everyone who had a pastoral simplicity in his early life had a haven of pleasant memories to which he could retreat from the horrors of city life. For some, the remembrances may well have been those of social isolation, economic hardship, and cultural deprivation. It is therefore possible that the concern of some reformers stemmed from a sincere desire to better farm life conditions.[18]

On the other hand, probably a great deal of the motivation of urban social workers who supported country life efforts came from alarm about the social consequences of rural decline and migration. For many of these people, there was the fear that rural ignorance and poverty with their attendant evils would become national problems to be added to existing city problems if something were not done to ameliorate them. As for migration to the cities, it contributed directly to problems of urban congestion and welfare by swelling the city population and by often adding new recipients of public aid. Rural welfare work thus offered these people a new channel or outlet for service. Moreover, in attempting to keep farmers on the land by making conditions more attractive, urban social workers were treating some of the city's problems at their source rather than working with their results.[19]

Concern about the influx of immigrants from southern Europe at the same time that the rural population was declining was another motivation of country life reformers. In particular, they worried about the impact these newcomers would have on the nation. Characterizing them as "illiterate, docile, lacking in self-reliance and initiative, and not possessing the Anglo-Teutonic conceptions of law, order, and government," rural uplifters attributed a variety of undesirable consequences to them.[20] One reformer declared, for example, that "their coming has served to dilute tremendously our national stock, and to corrupt our civic life."[21] Another believed that the admission of "indigestible foreign elements" weakened patrotism and caused a "confusion of morals, dearth of art and literature, and conflicts between classes."[22] Simultaneously, reform leaders argued, urbanization was causing Anglo-Saxon types to commit "race suicide" by restricting their birthrate. They therefore called for a cessation of the country exodus as a means to preserving men of native American stock on the land.[23]

But there was another problem which complicated this situation. Tenancy was increasing and attracting more and more immigrants. Not only was this a threat to the hope that native Americans in the country would balance off aliens in the cities, but it was also alleged to cause a deterioration of rural community life. Therefore, reformers wished to reverse the trend toward tenancy in order that a "cultured, progressive, liberal-minded people" be maintained on the land. The alternative, some argued, was for the rural districts to be populated by a "peasant-minded people whose interest in life, aside from the instinct of acquisition, is bounded by three elementary wants—hunger, thirst, and sex."[24]

Curiously, the Country Life Commission found during its investigation that many people commented favorably on immigrant labor. Indeed, it intended originally to include in its report a section discussing the indebtedness of American agriculture to immigrants and their superiority as farm hands. There was, however, strong protest from Commission-member Barrett, who insisted that most farmers in the South and West were opposed to the immigrant in agriculture. Perhaps this merely points up that not all people associated with the country life movement held racist attitudes. Neither, as George Mowry has noted, did reformers have a monopoly on racism.[25]

For some reformers, the motivation to support country life efforts seemed to derive from their faith in science. They recognized that change was inevitable and urged that it be controlled, channeled, and made efficient through the use of scientific methods. In their opinion, farming was inefficient and a brake on national progress. If farmers could be made more skillful, they reasoned, more could be produced, prices would go down, wages paid to labor would not need to be so high, and American manufacturers could more easily meet the competition of foreign producers. They emphasized that farming was a system that involved more than merely growing crops. Marketing, financing, soil fertility, and other problems were part of the new requirements in agriculture. Farmers, to be efficient, needed to listen to the botanist, the entomologist, and the agricultural chemist. They also needed to become businessmen who scientifically managed their enterprises.[26]

During the nineteenth century it had been futile to scold farmers for their wastefulness since the frontier offered its abundance even to the extravagant. But in the early twentieth century, those who advocated efficiency and scientific methods had a better chance of receiving a hearing because of the high cost of living and the fear of a shortage of food. For many Americans, wasteful farmers made excellent scapegoats.

Obviously, conservationists could see in the scientific aspects of the country life movement the same ideal of efficient utilization without waste which they held with respect to natural resources. In fact, many conservationists thought that soil fertility was the most important resource and the farmers the chief exploiters. They therefore enthusiastically supported efforts to combat this situation by making farmers the chief conservators.[27]

For certain economic groups, it was good business to help farmers make successes of their enterprises. Local merchants would gain sales and mail-order houses would enlarge their newly gained parcel post markets. Railroads would increase their farm shipping while bankers would gain in numbers of potential borrowers. It was probably not a coincidence that many of these businessmen were the same ones attacked by the Populists. No doubt these men desired to neutralize the agrarian radicalism which festered earlier. Some of these businessmen did, however, effectively promote scientific methods among farmers. Bankers, for example, wrote terms requiring the use of scientific techniques into loans or withheld loans if these terms were not agreeable.[28] Outstanding here, then, was a mixture of self-interest and concern for scientific efficiency.

Equally important with faith in science and efficiency as motivating factors behind the efforts of country life reformers was the belief in organization. According to Walter Hines Page, it was "the greatest invention in modern times and the greatest engine of all progress." Liberty Hyde Bailey felt it could uplift an individual "by developing the associative spirit in such a way that he may retain his own self-help at the same time that he secures the help of his fellows and the incentive of community action." Kenyon Butterfield saw organization as a means to strengthen community spirit and underscored its potential for social stimulation and response. In an era of organization of group interests, rural reformers wanted to help the farmer, the "separate, unattached man," become organized and many of them therefore preached a full-blown "gospel of cooperation, companionship and better farm life" for men on the land.[29]

A belief in something similar to the national integration envisioned by Herbert Croly and Theodore Roosevelt seemed to be yet another motivating factor. Like Roosevelt's insistence that the "national need" be placed "before sectional or personal advantage," country life leaders urged the adoption of a "national point of view." Bailey, Wallace, and others repeatedly exhorted country and city people to cooperate, arguing that human forces operated in both rural and urban life and they should not be separated. The country, they declared, needed the stimulation of city ideas, and the city could use the inspiration of country ideals.[30]

But it was probably the faith of reformers in the efficacy of education which most inspired them to support country life improvements. Indeed, for many, man's ability to dominate the forces of nature through an increased understanding of his environment was a faith almost as mystical as the belief in the power of rural life to transform mankind. The Country Life Commission characteristically noted in its report, for example, that "all difficulties resolve themselves in the end into a question of education." Charging that rural education was unimaginative and that it dealt too much with books, reformers insisted that it be changed to reflect the society in which it existed. Only in that way, they believed, would the "enlarged vision of the possibilities of country life" be promoted.[31]

Rural reform leaders, like the groups which they led as part of the country life movement, were a diverse lot with a variety of reasons for their involvement. Significantly, some of the same characteristics which others have found among leaders of the broader Progressive movement are distinguishable in the attitudes and viewpoints of rural life reformers.[32] Like Progres-

sives, country life leaders sometimes sought refuge in individualism, while at other times they firmly supported social-mindedness. A part of the agrarian leadership, despite its urban background, shared with some Progressives an attachment to the
past, when farmers had more status and prestige. On the other
hand, another part of the country life leadership, like other
Progressives, looked forward to a modern, dynamic state based
on scientific management, conservation, and efficiency. As with
Progressive thought, furthermore, there was a strain of racism
present in country life thinking. Many rural reformers, although
by no means all, also shared with Progressive leaders the same
mistrust of materialism. A stress on social integration through
collective organization was yet another characteristic of country
life efforts which many Progressives also emphasized. Moreover,
the Progressives' aversion to special privilege seen in their opposition to the trusts had a comparable, if less dramatic, manifestation among rural life reformers, who saw farmers as "disadvantaged" individuals in part because of the consequences of industrial concentration. Finally, the strong moralistic strain of
Progressivism was very evident among country life leaders.

*   *   *

Theodore Roosevelt was the leading national figure to support country life efforts. As with others in the movement, it
seems rather remarkable that he was concerned about agriculture and the farmers' welfare since his life, with the exception
of a brief ranching experience in the Dakota Territory, was spent
entirely in an urban environment. Born and reared in the nation's largest city and of an upper-class commercial family background, Roosevelt was "as truly a product of Old New York
as Henry Adams was of Old Boston."[33] Throughout his career
his associations were mostly with urban conditions, and he had
little contact with authentic rural America. The "farmers" he
knew best were gentlemen such as Austin Wadsworth, upon
whose New York estate he sometimes hunted.[34]

However, like other country life leaders, Roosevelt's concern
about the conditions of agriculture and rural life was motivated
by a number of factors. First of all, he had a genuine love of
nature and the outdoors, which gave him some sympathy with
country life and provided a springboard for both his concern
for rural reform and the conservation of resources. His fascina-

tion with natural science began in his youth, and when he entered Harvard he actually planned to become a naturalist. Although he gave up the idea and later entered politics, he retained his interest in nature, and during his lifetime he authored numerous books and articles on various aspects of natural history.[35]

Along with many of his contemporaries, Roosevelt also held certain notions regarding farming and farmers. Primary among these were his beliefs that agriculture was the basis of economic prosperity and that farmers were the embodiment of the virtues of individualism, independence, and industriousness which had made America great. He declared, in fact, that the greatness of any nation rested upon the character of its rural population more than anything else. Like Jefferson, he believed that the "farmer who owns his own farm" was the "preeminently typical American" who stood for fundamental American ideals and provided a necessary safeguard against dangerous social and political changes.[36] Even in an increasingly industrialized economy, he asserted, farmers continued to play a basic role by providing cheap foodstuffs and the raw materials processed by manufacturers.[37]

Another explanation of the President's solicitude for farmers was his alarm at the rapid drift of country people to the city and the dire implication this had for the "racial" composition of the American population in the future. Along with others living near the turn of the century, Roosevelt feared for the dominance of the "native American stock" as farm people migrated to the cities, where their birth rate tended to decrease, at the same time as immigration from southern and eastern Europe was increasing. The northern European ethnic background of most American farmers endeared them to Roosevelt, and he looked to them to produce the additional numbers necessary to offset the growing percentage of "unassimilable" newcomers in the population. Because he firmly believed that native American farmers were the superior people of the agrarian tradition, he wished to see their preponderance in the nation continued.[38]

Roosevelt was also appalled by the lack of any systematic management in public land policy. No doubt this was an aspect of the President's well-known interest in conservation, since he believed that land administration, like the management of other natural resources, needed professional leadership and efficient, scientific control. Placing great faith in applied science and modern technology, he insisted that waste, exploitation, and inefficiency could be eliminated by trained professionals who would undertake scientific investigations and arrive at workable solutions to existing problems. Therefore, throughout his years in office he repeatedly sought out men of science who could bring the knowledge and practices of their disciplines to bear on federal policies.[39]

Still another reason for Roosevelt's interest in rural matters was his apprehension about the ability of America to feed its growing population after the frontier "closed" and only a limited amount of land of diminishing fertility remained. The increasing rural exodus and his belief that the world was never more than a year from starvation probably added to his anxiety about this situation.[40] In any event, he came to support the use of scientific farming practices, the reclamation of arid regions through irrigation, and the withholding of public lands for actual homesteaders as ways to increase farm production. While he was President he therefore frequently praised the efforts of the Department of Agriculture to promote more efficient farming, and by the time he left office he was convinced that scientific agricultural training should be subsidized by the federal government.[41] Early in his administration, moreover, he gave vigorous personal support to the passage of the Newlands Act, which provided for reclamation of land through irrigation projects planned and financed by the federal government.[42] The President's wish to see public lands reserved for actual settlers, along with his desire for a more orderly land policy, prompted him to appoint a Public Lands Commission in 1903 to examine existing land laws and make recommendations for their reform. He extended his concern for the welfare of homesteaders still further when he urged that land reclaimed under the Newlands Act and the unsettled parts of Hawaii be reserved for farmers.[43]

Finally, there is some evidence that despite his upper-class, city-bred background, Roosevelt believed he was a champion of the farmer. Concerning himself and farmers, he wrote in 1903 that "for all the superficial differences between us, down at the bottom these men and I think a good deal alike, or at least have the same ideals."[44] Shortly after his inauguration in 1905 he wrote the English historian George Otto Trevelyan that the majority of his supporters in the previous year's election had been "Lincoln's plain people." They had voted for him, he thought, because they believed he was sympathetic to them and as devoted to their interests as he might have been if he had come from among their midst. "And," he continued, "I certainly feel that I do understand them and believe in them and feel for them and try to represent them."[45]

However, farmers were Theodore Roosevelt's last interest as they had been Jefferson's first. His thinking respecting the farmers' problems developed late and he did not, as President, initiate any remarkable changes for the improvement of agriculture. His concern with the social betterment of farmers was particularly slow developing, and during the early years of his administration he actually thought farm life pleasant for farmers, all things considered. It was only near the end of his second term, when he was about to leave office, that he gave much attention to the amelioration of rural social conditions.[46]

Once he became interested in farm problems, however, Roosevelt took an essentially contradictory approach to remedying them. On the one hand, he stressed that farmers could resolve their difficulties only through their own hard work, initiative, and intelligence. But on the other hand, he advocated and even gave federal aid to farmers and encouraged them to organize to promote their interests. Obviously, the independence and initiative Roosevelt so much admired about farmers could not be preserved in the face of expanded governmental action or farmer organization. He tried to reconcile these positions by insisting that government assistance was "to help farmers to help themselves" and by declaring that cooperative interaction need not infringe the farmers' independence.[47] However, it was an inescapable fact that it did, and Roosevelt simply could not have the best of both arguments.

Actually, the President's dilemma was the dilemma of the country life movement. Like the dichotomous groups in the movement, he tried to face in two directions at once, looking backward to a largely mythical Arcadia of simple rusticism and forward to a twentieth-century society in which farmers would need to rely on scientific efficiency and business practices to succeed. He was President, of course, during a time of transition, and his thought tended to mingle the old with the new. He not only carried over into his thinking some of the traditional frontier ideas and attitudes, but he also sensed the demands of a new industrial age and emphasized the need for scientific procedure, organization, and a greater degree of social control. It was therefore possible for some people to see him as a Jeffersonian carrying out the basic prescriptions of Populism, while others could regard him as a Hamiltonian lacking any real social goals and advocating expanded governmental action.[48]

chapter four

Liberty Hyde Bailey, Philosopher of Country Life

Despite Theodore Roosevelt's national leadership, the personality of Liberty Hyde Bailey looms largest in the history of the country life movement during the opening decades of the twentieth century. Both his contemporaries and more recent writers agree on this point.[1] A representative figure in the movement, he combined in his career most of the characteristics of rural reform leadership identified in the preceding chapter.

Born on a Michigan farm in 1858, graduated from Michigan Agricultural College, and given further training in botany by Asa Gray at Harvard, Bailey gained a national reputation as a teacher and administrator in the agricultural college at Cornell University, as an author and editor of numerous publications, and as a spokesman for country life reform. Highly imaginative and a lover of nature, he was an agrarian sentimentalist who earnestly emphasized the older virtues of simplicity and individualism. At the same time, he was a scientist who recognized, although somewhat grudgingly, that change and organization were necessary aspects of modern life. His love of nature prompted his ardent support of conservationist policies, while his scientific training and academic background encouraged his belief that education provided the primary solution to rural life problems.[2]

Bailey's concern about country life matters began early in his career, and his influence upon rural developments during his lifetime was manifold. Even before the turn of the century he expressed the view that the social as well as the economic welfare of farmers needed studying, and with colleagues at Cornell he initiated the use of the survey as a method for gathering information about the farm situation.[3] While at Cornell he also pioneered the offering of farm-extension services, which attempted to make the findings of science available and practical for agriculturists through lectures, leaflets, and demonstrations.[4] Similarly, he actively supported the turn-of-the-century nature-study movement, which he viewed as a means for inculcating love of country living in rural children.[5] In addition, Bailey, along with Kenyon Butterfield, was an early promoter of the inclusion of agricultural economics, rural sociology, and home economics as disciplines in the curriculum of agricultural colleges.[6] As already noted, Bailey perfomed a singular service when he served as chairman of the Country Life Commission in 1908, since under his direction the commissioners fashioned a report which set down, although in general terms, a pattern for rural advancement. But despite all these accomplishments, Bailey's greatest impact upon rural reform was as the philosopher of American country life, for he was a prolific writer whose works were widely read in both the city and the country and he doubtlessly inspired many people with his love of nature and rural living.[7] Moreover, his concern for social, economic, and technical problems confronting the agricultural community qualified him as a sympathetic farm spokesman. It therefore seems appropriate to consider his thought for the additional understanding it may provide as to the nature of country life leadership.

* * *

Liberty Hyde Bailey possessed a philosophy of country life in which he envisioned a new rural civilization based, above all else, on the concern of men for nature. He was convinced that many of the annoying problems of the early twentieth century were traceable to the disregard for nature of his contemporaries. Sympathy with nature was fundamental to successful living, he maintained, and this required knowledge of the physical aspects and other phenomena of one's surroundings. Unless the mind were sensitive to these things, neither satisfying living nor efficient farming was possible. "Good farmers are good naturalists," he wrote. Rural reformers, he believed, tended to ignore this necessary development of nature-love among agriculturists, and they therefore misguidedly started with plans for social and economic organization.[8]

Extremely romantic, Bailey had an abiding faith in the reforming effect of developing in farmers a spiritual attitude toward nature. He was convinced that if farmers understood the processes of nature, they would find farming just as interesting and satisfying as any other occupation. Such an understanding would stimulate their interest in their work, make it more enjoyable, and increase their production. But most importantly, the knowledge that they were cooperating with nature would create an appreciation of the natural world about them and stimulate uplifting spiritual qualities in their lives.[9]

It was not farmers alone who needed an understanding and appreciation of nature; Bailey advocated a return to nature during moments of relaxation for everyone. He recognized that this would not cure the ills of contemporary civilization, but he felt it would restore "proper balance and proportion" to life. "If it were possible for every person to own a tree and to care for it," he wrote, "the good results would be beyond estimation." Moreover, Bailey saw in the growing suburban development, the increased vacationing in the country, and the growing number of books on nature subjects, an indication that many people desired to get back to nature and the outdoors. There was, he believed, a genuine need for more parks and nature preserves.[10]

To Bailey, nature was inherently good and he therefore disliked the expression "bad weather." It was mainly the fear of soiling one's clothing, he believed. "Weather is not a human institution, and therefore it cannot be 'bad'," he wrote. He also had an unusual attitude toward weeds. Ignoring their pest qualities, he simply viewed them as plants in which he was interested and for a time he even had a "weed garden" in his backyard. Similarly, he did not like to hear people refer to their love for flowers since such blossoms were only part of a plant and it was the plants they should love. A plant, he rhapsodized, was a living, growing thing, a companion; but a flower was merely an ornament, something for a vase or a buttonhole.[11]

While Bailey was director of the Agricultural College at Cornell, there was some criticism leveled at extension bulletins which concerned flower growing. Such bulletins were suitable for florists, the critics maintained, but farmers wanted information on how to grow cabbages and other crops. Bailey replied that instruction in flower culture was needed by farmers to increase the attractiveness and interest of country life. Flowers, he believed, could bring delight to otherwise drab lives and help lift up the spirits of farmers as they went wearily about their daily chores. For this reason, he did not think agricultural colleges and experiment stations should restrict their work exclusively to the so-called practical or economic side of farming.[12]

Bailey was also an exponent of the cult of simplicity. The sincerity, unpretensiousness, and simplicity of country folk endeared them to him and he believed that people everywhere needed to retain commonplace, yet artistic, expressions of life. It was especially necessary for people to do this at a time when life was becoming increasingly complex. "Certain it is," he wrote, "that every sensitive soul feels this longing for something that is elemental in the midst of the voluminous and intricate, something free and natural that shall lie close to the heart and really satisfy his best desires."[13]

It would seem from the foregoing that Bailey was not at ease in a modern America which was getting more and more complex, noisy, hurried, and exacting. To some extent, this was true. However, he apparently did not wish to undo technological progress but only desired the retention of older values. He considered many contemporary developments a "clear gain to the world" because they maintained efficiency, but at the same time he believed a simpler attitude toward life, a kind of spiritual temperament, was needed. How to have both the new and the old was the critical problem, and it is a premise underlying this study that it was impossible to have both simultaneously. Some people recognized this at the time, but Liberty Hyde Bailey and many country life leaders were not among them.[14]

Despite his scientific training, Bailey had a strong sentimental attachment to a romanticized version of the agrarian tradition, and its major themes are repeated again and again in his writings. He was convinced that farmers were "the fundamental fact in democracy." Indeed, they were "background people," the bedrock elements upon which any viable society had to rest. "As the land-people live and have their being, so will our civic and social life be conditioned and sustained," he wrote. And he believed so firmly in this that he was not sure a purely urban civilization could ever exist, since city life needed to be constantly renewed "from vitalities in the rear." Bailey concluded, moreover, that rural life had always been and would always be superior to any urban existence. To him, farming was a joyful privilege and a holy trusteeship for the administration of one of nature's important resources, the land, and he bitterly resented the inference that it was chiefly struggle and hardship.[15]

The same reverence which characterized Bailey's feelings toward nature therefore pervaded his thinking about the land. He believed that the earth was "holy" because it was part of the creation and the basis of life for mankind. Since the earth was holy, he resolved, all things which grew out of it were also holy. Therefore, the first obligation of everyone in each generation was to respect the land and keep it "artistically fit." Bailey even suggested that international conferences be held to discuss the best ways to maintain the land "clean and productive and sweet for the good of mankind." And he proposed that "a Society of the Holy Earth" be established with love of the soil as the bond holding it together. The ultimate good that came from contact with the land, he believed, was the moral development of the people involved. "One does not act rightly toward one's fellows if one does not know how to act rightly toward the earth," he wrote. More people ought therefore to have an opportunity to own and use the land.[16]

Since Bailey believed that farmers were engaged in a quasi-public business, he recognized the logic in the argument that it might become necessary to regulate them in their treatment of the soil. He preferred, however, to see men made responsible without resort to "the crudities of legislation," and he proposed several alternatives to laws to protect soil fertility. He suggested, for example, that if land fell into decline or if the owner was not keeping it up, the state should buy it and either convert it to large, manageable farms operated by the government, or it should sell the land to farmers who would keep it properly. Because tenants so often did not recognize the public interest in soil fertility, he suggested that they either be given the opportunity to own land or be obligated by contract to fertilize the soil and look more rigorously after its general upkeep.[17]

A concomitant of Bailey's agrarian bias was his antiurbanism. To him, cities were elaborate and artificial creations in contrast to the country, which was natural and direct. Men in the cities were pathetically troubled and uneasy creatures, he believed, because they were separated from nature and the land. Moreover, as noted earlier, Bailey considered cities parasitic and dependent. "Cut off the traffic in milk and water and other supplies from the country for twenty-four hours," he declared in terms reminiscent of William Jennings Bryan, and the city "will be in despair." But "annihilate the cities," he continued, "and the country still exists; and I should not marvel if it would be a month before some of the countrymen would hear of the phenomenon."[18]

In his numerous books and articles Bailey indicted much of contemporary urban life: the impersonality, the lack of artistry in anything, the price tags on everything, the hurried pace of the people, and the overwhelming preoccupation with money and materialism. In the cities, moreover, there was too much love of ease and pleasure, which tended to breed weakness and evasion of duty. And the urban extravagance with time and money was to Bailey a clear manifestation of the wastefulness of human energy in the city environment. He wrote, "I marvel at the enormous waste of human effort, and at the insincerity and indirection; and I wonder what might be the state of civilization were half of this energy and shrewd ingenuity to be applied to effort that would make for usefulness."[19]

Bailey's social theory was another derivative of his agrarianism. As he saw society, it moved between two poles: at one extreme were "the syndicated and corporate interests," while at the other was "the laboring class." Both of these groups were lawless by nature, the one because it had laws made in its own behalf, the other because it took the law into its own hands. Bailey thought that "the great land-owning and land-working class," which was stable, conservative, and law-abiding, stood between these two and served as a "balance-force or middle wheel of society." Farmers were, he believed, a greater stabilizing influence in society than most people realized.[20]

Like the Progressives whom George Mowry studied, Bailey was very antimaterialistic. Some of this was perhaps a reaction to the deference which contemporary society seemed to pay to commercial success while scorning professors, authors, and other intellectuals as "impractical" men whose statements should be ignored. But part of the explanation was undoubtedly Bailey's great concern with the spiritual side of life. From his viewpoint, men spent too much time magnifying limited materialistic goals and thereby neglected the more significant aspects of living. "Trade is a small part of life," he wrote. "Man's existence lies mostly beyond the ledger; life is not a pocketbook!" Some of the income from farming, for example, was psychic, deriving from the joy of everyday living on the farm with all of its sights, sounds, and fragrances. The tendency to make farming merely a business, and to talk of it primarily in commercial terms, was, to Bailey, a mistake and one aspect of the contemporary malaise. Agriculture, for him, was not just a technical occupation nor merely an enterprise, but it was a civilization, for farmers were concerned not only with production, distribution, and selling, but also with the making of homes on the land.[21]

He was convinced that it was not sufficient to be comfortable and make money. Life required more than that; it needed spiritual satisfactions and art. Bailey insisted that the great gains in this world came not from personal advantage but from such things as service to one's fellow man and from making something purely for the love of it. Life also needed beauty, and for farmers this meant better maintenance of fields, roadsides, barnyards, and premises in general. "We need," he declared, "to transfer some of the stress of our teaching from commercial ends to the productive habit of attractiveness."[22]

Perhaps above all else, Bailey was a moralist. His strictures on the developments of his day depict unbridled paganism, a pervasive lack of respect, and mad movement after money and possessions. He believed that people had forgotten nature and simplicity in their restless search for new excitement and pleasure and he urged them to recognize the innate goodness of nature and the benefits to be gained from simple experiences. "We should try to find meanings rather than to be satisfied only with the spectacles," he wrote.[23]

With specific reference to the problems of the early twen-

tieth century, Bailey believed that the great urban centers had
encouraged combinations which had become abusive, with a few
attempting to exploit the many. This happened largely because
society had not provided "guiding and correcting measures."
Bailey therefore proposed two ways to reform this situation:
attempt to make men "personally honest and responsible," and
try to even up society "so that all men may have something like
a natural opportunity."[24]

An outgrowth of Bailey's moralism was his emphasis on
public service—"fellow-service," he called it. "No person should
be allowed to grow up without definite training for service," he
declared, for he believed that all men needed to develop sympathy and responsibility with respect to their fellow man. The contemporary reaction against "the grasping millionaire or trust"
and local efforts in support of improvement and better government convinced Bailey, moreover, that the idea of service was
gaining ground during the early years of the century.[25]

Interestingly, Bailey's intense feelings of humanitarianism
and social service were intimately bound up with a deep-seated
pacifism which was an integral part of his character. In 1877
when he entered Michigan Agricultural College, he prepared to
leave when he learned that military training was required of all
students at land grant institutions, but a sympathetic professor
interceded and had him assigned to laboratory work in place of
drill. Bailey was not a Quaker, but his attitude toward war and
military activities was apparently based on strong moral considerations. One of his biographers has suggested that possibly the
linking of his mother's death when he was not yet five years old
with the incessant talk of the struggle between the states caused
his lifelong aversion to war. Whatever the reason, Bailey never
lost his pacifistic idealism, although he did temper it somewhat
during the First World War, when he endorsed Theodore Roosevelt's preparedness position and wrote that "it is the obligation of
every able-bodied man to be his own soldier, when soldiering is
necessary." Even then, he expressed at the same time the hope
that the day would soon arrive when mankind would pass from
the "gunpowder stage into the fellowship stage." When that time
arrived he hoped the concept of cooperative effort so important
to military service would be employed for other, more constructive purposes.[26]

Bailey agreed with Theodore Roosevelt that when mankind ceased to contend it lost its virility, or, in a Rooseveltian term, "the fighting edge," but he did not accept Roosevelt's conclusion that the struggle had to be military. Rather, Bailey envisioned a social brotherhood of mankind struggling with nature. "We have scarcely begun even the physical conquest of the earth," he wrote. "There are mountains to pierce, seashores to reclaim, vast stretches of submerged land to drain, millions of acres to irrigate and many more millions to utilize by dry farming, rivers to canalize, the whole open country to organize and subdue." And, he continued, all this could call forth "the finest spirit of conquest" and would contribute at the same time to "the training of men and women."[27]

Despite Bailey's belief that the farmers' individualism and independence should be preserved, his contrary views concerning fellow-service apparently caused him to favor cooperative action among agriculturists. Like Roosevelt, he seemed to think that there could be organizations of farmers in which every member would still possess his freedom of action and be his own master. Neither man apparently recognized a contradiction here, that a member's independence of action was necessarily curtailed by the organization of which he was a part.[28]

Bailey, however, never unqualifiedly accepted the group impulse which was becoming predominant in American development. He objected, for example, to the proposal that farmers organize for commercial advantages because he believed that would only set one part of society against another whereas he looked forward to the time when antagonism based on different interests would be eliminated. "I have preferred even that the rural interests undergo disadvantages," he stated, "rather than that we throw agriculture into the maelstrom." He hoped society would provide economic safeguards for farmers which would make permanent organization unnecessary. He also believed the government should educate farmers, for with the proper knowledge, they could work out their own solutions individually. Bailey was essentially conservative, and it saddened him to see groups organize and use strikes, boycotts, and other devices to protect their interests. On the other hand, he recognized that fair treatment "should be theirs by right and by public regulation," and it was not.[29]

Bailey therefore interpreted cooperation among farmers in broader terms than mere business unity. To him, it included "everything that develops the common commercial, intellectual, recreative, and spiritual interests of the rural people." Redirection of rural society was the final goal Bailey envisioned, and he recognized the necessity of combined efforts on the part of the country people themselves in achieving some of the ends he had in mind. Moreover, he was aware that farmers, despite their individualism, were social beings who increasingly interacted with others in a world which had grown more interdependent, and some cooperative action would therefore be inevitable. According to Bailey, however, voluntarism should be the key aspect in the farmers' efforts. In addition, he cautioned that the government should not be involved and that the majority of rural people should support cooperative activities.[30]

Fear of the centralization of power and control was closely related to Bailey's concern about organization, because in it he recognized another threat to individualism. For Bailey, centralization simply involved too much regulation which seriously restricted local and individual initiative. He was also distressed by the way in which Americans seemed to equate centralization with efficiency and he could not understand, for example, why agricultural projects in New York and California should be approved in Washington. In his opinion, that did not increase efficiency since it seemed more efficient, and reasonable, to have those who handled the funds also administer the program.[31]

Further evidence of his concern about centralization can be seen in his response to the proposal to federate all groups involved in the country life movement. While he gave tentative approval to the idea, he was fearful that too much control and partisanship would soon become the dominant features of such an organization. As time passed he became more and more hesitant to support the proposal despite the fact that Butterfield and other rural leaders were enthusiastically working for it.[32]

An interesting aspect of Bailey's attitude toward centralizing tendencies which were being accepted during the years near the turn of the century is revealed in his views concerning nationalism and the proposal for a world government. He disagreed with those who deplored nationalism and wished to establish a League of Nations, because he believed the world government idea merely represented a supercentralization which might easily become a supertyranny. It was better, he thought, to work to remove the "blind prejudice, the over-organization, the self-interest for territory and gold" from nationalism. Then, even with centralized control, there would be "a political system for common betterment, a community of ideals, concrete enthusiasms, a means of effective training, racial and geographic cohesions, and programs to direct the lives of people."[33]

In discussing Bailey's agrarianism, his love of nature, and his moralism, it is easy to lose sight of the fact that he was, after all, a scientist and that his training undoubtedly influenced his thought. As a plant scientist, Bailey believed in evolution and the Darwinist position, since it stressed strength and power and rested process of adaptability. For this reason he rejected the Social Darwinist position, since it stressed strength and power and rested on a human analogy which he believed stemmed from a superficial observation of nature. There was no war in nature, he declared, and to fashion such analogies for the commercial world was deception. "The whole contrivance of nature is to protect the weak," he maintained. Men were inaccurate in their view of the "struggle in nature" and they gave it an "intensely human application." They needed to read Darwin more closely, for he used the term "struggle for existence" in a broad, metaphysical sense which included dependence of one being on another. What took place in nature, Bailey argued, was not some test of strength or a "contest in ambition," but rather a process of adjustment. Therefore, the real criterion of fitness in nature was adaptation, not power. Besides, he pointed out, human struggle should not be equated with animal behavior, which was admittedly on a lower plane, for to do so was to put man back on a level with creatures he was supposed to have passed in his development![34]

When it came to reconciling evolution with religious faith, Bailey took the somewhat deistic position that God created the universe, but evolution was the story of the changes which followed. Therefore, he understandably rejected orthodox religious belief and supported the "social gospel" conclusion that a viable religion should be based on constructive work in society rather than on doctrines. Moreover, he believed that religion should not rest on fear. If man were a part of nature and had evolved through natural processes, he reasoned, then he should feel a union with nature and not a fear of it. He was confident, however, that as men mastered the forces of nature, they would gain the courage necessary to eliminate fear and replace it with a spirit of fellowship with nature.[35]

Scientific training also conditioned Bailey's response to the age-old superstitions which abounded in many agricultural areas: crops had to be planted in the right phase of the moon, sheep fleeces would not be so heavy if sheared when the moon was waning, and so on. While Bailey enjoyed collecting these beliefs —examples of "moon-farming" he called them—he insisted that agricultural methods ought to be based on facts and not suppositions. Whether the moon exerted an influence over plants and animals was a matter to be determined by research, not by assumption. The time had arrived, he declared repeatedly, for farmers to stop consulting "the zodiac and the moon" and to use those things which could be scientifically proved.[36]

Both Bailey's scientific background and his intense love of nature promoted his interest in conservation matters. Like Sir Horace Plunkett and other country life leaders who were active in conservation efforts, Bailey believed conservation began with the men on the land. The problem was chiefly one of arousing their sense of responsibility so that they would feel they must leave the land at least as fertile as when they found it. Moreover, they had to be made to understand that freedom to use the land was not unlimited and that there was no inalienable right to ownership of land for there was always the obligation to conserve it for those generations yet unborn. To create this feeling of responsibility among farmers, he believed it was necessary to give them "a better understanding of the powers of the soil and the means of conserving them." Bailey therefore advocated agricultural education which would give farmers the knowledge required to permit them to properly conserve the nation's most important resource.[37]

Like most people in the country life movement and the broader Progressive reform effort, Bailey had an unlimited faith in education as a curative for contemporary problems. Specifically, he believed the country school could become the most dynamic force to be utilized in solving the many-sided rural problem if it were changed sufficiently. However, Bailey contended that the rural school as it then existed was not performing its basic function, which was to fit rural pupils for country life. To support this assertion, he referred to a study made of farm children in New Jersey which revealed that at age seven, twenty-six percent planned to follow rural occupations, but by the time they reached age fourteen, only two percent still hoped to be farmers.[38]

A large part of the problem with the country school, Bailey believed, was the excessive attention it gave to books and abstract subjects and the "dry" teaching which was bound too much to the "pouring-in-and-dipping-out process" of education. It needed to have more vital contact with the life around it and to teach in terms of the pupil's experience. Changed in this way, the country school would give motivation to farm youth and teach them the beauty as well as the profit of farming. Moreover, it would demonstrate that intellectual growth, culture, and social enjoyment were eminently possible in rural life. If, as Bailey believed, a goal of rural education was to prepare country men and women for life, the school could do this best by teaching pupils to idealize everything with which they came in contact during their day-to-day existence.[39]

Bailey thought effective teaching in country schools should concern things and not study about things. If pupils studied corn, for example, they should handle corn in order to make their own observations. Similarly, when they studied farm animals, they should actually see them and not merely relate what someone said about them. Bailey also objected to the "sit-still-and-keep-still" method of school discipline, and he wanted schools without "screwed-down seats" in which children would be put to work "with tools and soils and plants and problems." He recognized that healthy, growing children were active children and he therefore wanted rural schools to have rooms where projects could be worked on and displayed by pupils. But, he stressed, even a bustling schoolroom was to be viewed as merely an annex to the outdoors, where field trips should be conducted and gardens planted to give children the firsthand experience of knowing nature and growing things.[40]

It was Bailey's opinion that education should always start with the pupils and their environment, and in rural areas that meant it should begin with nature. He therefore emphasized nature study, and while he was at Cornell he established a broad program of nature study training. John W. Spencer, a New York fruit grower and nature enthusiast, Anna Botsford Comstock, Ada Georgia, Mary Rogers Miller, and Alice McClosky, all dedicated teachers, idealists, and organizers, aided him in his efforts. As its major activity, the group issued a series of leaflets for teachers and pupils, while Spencer spearheaded the organization of hundreds of Junior Naturalist Clubs. Bailey, for his part, authored some of the leaflets and was tireless in his warnings to teachers not to stress technical aspects which would be foreign to the pupil's experience, for nature study was not a science, but an attitude, "a point of view." Since it was not a precise discipline, there was no reason to teach exact details which could come later in traditional science courses.[41]

Nature study, Bailey stressed repeatedly, was a form of learning that could not be set off from the rest of the curriculum, which meant that all school subjects should be taught in terms of the environment as much as possible. Geography, for example, might concern the hills, valleys, and streams in the rural area, while arithmetic could be taught in terms of problems in land and crop measurement. History, meanwhile, could be presented with reference to settlement of the local area, and so on for all subjects. Bailey believed that after pupils had been interested in their immediate environment, they could then be taken out to the broader world beyond.[42]

Through interesting the child in nature, Bailey hoped to change rural attitudes toward the farm by bringing country children into sympathy with their environment. "Only as we love the country is country life worth living," he wrote. Science and the business side of farming were important, but they did not need emphasis at this formative level; a sensitive interest in the outdoors was more important in the elementary grades. Properly undertaken, nature study would inspire farm youth with the joy of living in the country and would affect their attitudes toward their circumstances and their fellowmen as well. In the end, Bailey believed, it was nature study which would promote the required point of view among farmers, for children who studied God's work firsthand would never desire the artificialities of city life.[43]

Bailey did believe, however, that agriculture should be taught later in the school program, but he did not think that it should be the exclusively technical agricultural training offered in the land grant colleges. "I hope no country life teaching will be so narrow as to put only technical farm subjects before the pupil," he stated. What he proposed were courses in agricultural economics and rural sociology, and he believed the day would arrive when such courses would have greater impact on the advancement of rural life than the teaching of technical agriculture. This new kind of teaching would awaken and nourish the spiritual side of farm life, causing farmers to be more responsive to social amenities such as attractive and comfortable homes, better reading, music, and art. He did recognize that the economic side of farming had to receive some attention in order for farmers to have more money with which to buy these creature comforts, but at the same time he pointed out that increased income did not itself awaken a desire for them.[44]

However, agricultural education during the years near the turn of the century was not systematized. Courses ranged from the study of botany, chemistry, and other technical aspects of agriculture to some pioneering efforts to teach rural economics and sociology. Moreover, agricultural subjects were being added, sometimes haphazardly, to the curriculum of public schools, normal schools, colleges, and universities, and occasionally even specialized agricultural schools were being established. Bailey criticized these tendencies because they promoted duplication and lacked any organized plan. In curious contrast to his antipathy toward centralization in other areas, he recommended a nationalized program of educational coordination. "It is most unusual that in a country in which education is said to amount to a religion, there should be so little coordination at Washington," he wrote. Specifically, Bailey proposed that the Bureau of Education be enlarged and reconstituted as a Department of Education to fulfill this need. It was probably not coincidence that in 1909 the idea, along with several others held by the Country Life Commission chairman, found its way into the commission's report.[45]

It irritated Bailey to have people make a distinction between a so-called "liberal" education and one in agriculture which stressed technical training. In his opinion there was "as much culture in the study of beet roots as in the study of Greek roots," and he fairly bristled at the remark of a president of a liberal arts college that his school "educated men, not farmers and blacksmiths." Throughout his tenure at Cornell he had to contend with professors of literature, language, and law who looked upon agriculture as a poor academic relative and could see no connection between a dairy barn on campus and education. The prejudice against agricultural courses existed even among the rural population, for a farm mother once told Bailey that her husband wanted their son to attend an agricultural college but that she wanted him "to get an education." Bailey believed that any intellectual activity, whatever its application, promoted mental growth and power and therefore agriculture was an entirely legitimate subject in a high school or college curriculum.[46]

Education, Bailey believed, was not confined to formal course work in school but comprised all experience and training, with many agencies and institutions contributing to it. One of these "agencies" which Bailey pioneered, as noted earlier, was the "extension" idea of the agricultural colleges, whereby they offered education to the farm population through demonstration work, reading courses, surveys, and so on. A good extension program, Bailey suggested, should also utilize the experience of successful farmers and make more use of agricultural fairs. He emphasized, however, that the central purpose of all these efforts should be to help rural people solve their own problems by permitting them to see what scientific methods could do and then allowing them to take whatever action they chose.[47]

While Bailey's educational reform proposals may seem either outmoded or commonplace today, they were remarkably advanced during the years near the dawn of the century. Moreover, they bear a striking resemblance to ideas which John Dewey was developing independently at the same time. Perhaps most obvious is the fact that both men considered the school a part of society and not separate from the environment in which it existed. They believed, in addition, that the school should be a place of activity rather than one where pupils spent their time routinely memorizing and reciting lessons. Both stressed, furthermore, that the educational process should take place within an atmosphere of love and rapport and not in one of fear and formality. Both men also concluded that a child's education should start from the place where he happened to be in his development rather than from an arbitrary beginning point set for all children. Bailey and

Dewey also shared a common objection to the traditional attitude that people with liberal educations were "educated" whereas farmers and mechanics were merely "trained." The two men agreed, moreover, that nature study was important although their reasons were quite different: for Bailey it was needed to inculcate love of country life, while for Dewey it was to be used to teach elements of science. Finally, both thought the American educational system had "grown from the top down" rather than from the grassroots as it should have developed.[48]

*   *   *

Liberty Hyde Bailey's philosophy of country life stemmed from a sensitive response to the forces of nature much more than from any deep contemplation of the contemporary problems facing farmers. An agrarian sentimentalist with an unbounded faith in the goodness of nature, he possessed a profound love for the rural environment. Therefore, when he assessed the rural situation of his day he concluded that the chief problem was how to make farmers revere all things rural. Education was the best way to do this, he decided, since country children could be taught to love their environment by the introduction of nature study into the rural school curriculum.

However, Bailey's agrarian sentimentalism and fondness for the rural past seemed to obscure much of his view of the present and his vision of the future. From his comments on the farmers' situation, it is apparent that he failed to give proper recognition to farm problems inherent in the adjustment of agriculture to the new industrial age. He was not alone in this faulty analysis, however, for many country life leaders also believed that farmers could keep pace with the economy by accepting the tools and practices of the new era without sacrificing their independence of mind, self-reliance, and the virtues supposedly derived from living close to the soil. But by believing and wishing otherwise, Bailey and country life reformers could not change the fact that realities brought into existence by the commercialization of agriculture tended to contradict their romanticized concept of the farmers' uniqueness.

chapter five

The "Rural Problem," 1900–1920:
Analysis and Remedy

Measured by historical standards, agriculture was unquestionably more successful during the opening decades of the twentieth century than it had ever been in the past. Yet people in the country life movement insisted that farm life had certain deficiencies and inequities which made it unsatisfying. They believed that an adequate rural civilization had to be evaluated in terms of its possibilities rather than simply by comparison with previous conditions. Therefore, an examination of the reformers' analyses and suggested solutions to the multifaceted "rural problem" seems called for in order to shed more light on the rationale underlying reform efforts.

Probably the *Report of the Country Life Commission,* the official statement of the movement, is a logical place to begin the discussion since it incorporated most of the points of the reformers' critique in one succinct statement. On the whole, the *Report* asserted, agriculture in the United States was prosperous but it had not kept pace with industrial development, and this in turn affected the whole fabric of rural society. In particular, farm life suffered from marked social inadequacies which left it dissatisfying. The *Report* declared, however, that that stemmed from the farmers' failure to adjust to the fundamental change from an agriculturally based economy with its concept of individualism to an industrially centered one with its principle of organization of interests. Farmers remained unorganized and suffered inequalities and even injustices as a result. Some of these disadvantages, the *Report* continued, resulted from speculative landholding and the monopolistic control and wastage of streams and forested areas. Others were due to restraints on trade, lack of good roads, soil depletion, shortages of labor, inadequate sanitation facilities, and the deplorable condition of women's work on the farm. A number of these shortcomings had been discussed by the agricultural press and farm groups long before the turn of the century, but others were the result of the more recent industrialization of the economy and the commercialization of agriculture.[1]

Selfish speculation in land, the *Report* stated, denied to cultivators tillable acres which they might otherwise have obtained. In a similar way, control of streams and rivers by consolidated interests threatened rural welfare by depriving agriculturists of the use of these resources for cheap transportation, power sources, drainage lines, and irrigation. As for the exploitation of forested areas by private concerns, the *Report* affirmed that it reduced timber reserves valuable to the rural population, caused disastrous soil erosion, exposed farming areas to flooding, and ruined streams for navigation and other uses. Restraint of trade, which referred to alleged abuses of and discriminations toward farmers by transportation companies and middlemen, recalled Populist dissatisfaction of an earlier era. The dearth of good roads related to obvious economic and social disadvantages such as the inability to carry produce to market at times when prices were best and the difficulty of intercommunity socializing. Declining soil fertility due to poor farming, the *Report* declared, influenced the men on the land by bringing "poverty and degradation" in the form of a miserable system of tenantry, spiritual demoralization, and political impotence. Moreover, the scarcity of farm labor caused largely by urban industrial demands and agriculture's inability to compete for workers in terms of year-round employment, wages, and working conditions, handicapped farmers in the effective operation of their enterprises. As to the inadequate provision for health protection and the lack of enough doctors and sanitation authorities, the *Report* stated that these conditions were very harmful to both the public and private well-being of rural residents. Finally, the *Report* demanded that the situation of farm women, upon whom the monotony and loneliness of country life rested most heavily, be given sympathetic attention.[2]

Remedies for each of these problems were recommended by the *Report*. To protect the "inherent rights of land workers," the federal government was urged to act, although it was not made clear exactly what it should do that would be effective. The only recommendations the *Report* offered were that the government extend rural mail service, establish parcel post and postal savings systems, conduct a "thoroughgoing" investigation of business practices related to the farmers' welfare, and remember agriculturists when framing legislation. To eliminate grievances of the rural community against the common carriers, a subject treated cautiously by the authors of the *Report,* it was proposed only that better understanding be promoted between farmers and transportation companies. As to middlemen, a "searching inquiry" into their activities was suggested before any public action was taken. To solve the road problem, the *Report* recommended that the federal government establish a highway engineering service to advise the states on road building and upkeep. Adoption of "a system of diversified and rotation farming" was suggested by the *Report* as the way to halt "soil mining," while shorter hours and improved working and living conditions were called for as a means to attract farm labor. The teaching of hygiene and sanitation principles in the public schools was recommended to improve the health of the country population, but the *Report* also urged that the states more closely supervise health and sanitation in rural districts and that the federal government be permitted to send its health officials into the states upon the request of state governments. To lighten the work of farm women, the *Report* recommended a more helpful, cooperative spirit in the farm family and additional household conveniences; to relieve the monotony and isolation of their lives, it urged the acquisition of telephones and the creation of more women's organizations.[3]

In addition, certain basic "corrective forces" needed to be set in motion if country life were to realize all its possibilities. First, there should be improvement of community and social life through a series of surveys which would show resources available in rural areas as well as those which were lacking. Second, a redirected education should be established to promote satisfaction with country living and competency in modern agriculture. Third, cooperative organization was needed among farm people to forward their economic and social interests. Fourth, an institutionalized church was required to exert a necessary social influence as well as a spiritual one. Finally, and most importantly, there would have to be a voluntary response from those living in the agricultural community to participate in the upbuilding of rural civilization.[4]

The *Report* may be called the great manifesto of the country life movement, but it can hardly be compared favorably with such resounding calls to arms of the past as those of Marx and Engels in 1848 or the Populist Party in 1892. For the most part, it contained unspecific statements and conclusions, lacked forceful language, and failed to demand immediate state or federal action to solve existing problems. Its tone was subdued and conservative in nature. Moreover, the commission's belief that remedies were "of many kinds, and they must come slowly" reflected the cautiousness and moderation of the country life movement in general. Like others in the movement, the authors of the *Report* were hesitant to seek governmental assistance except in those instances where abuses seemed unreasonable and resolvable only by governmental action. Although some issues discussed by the commission were obviously economic, the commissioners seemed to reduce most questions to moral terms, which they felt could not be legislated. In large part, the solutions were to be found in education.[5]

Despite the fact that the *Report* was no ringing call to crusaders for farm betterment, it did give a general pronouncement on the rural situation and an impetus to propagandizing efforts. During the half dozen or so years after it was issued, hundreds of articles and books were written covering all phases of the rural problem. Moreover, farm magazines and newspapers increased their advertising of "septic tanks, central heating systems, deep well pumps, electric lighting plants for the home, and power washing machines." Of course, the accelerating migration of country people to the city throughout the period probably had much to do with the sense of urgency involved in these attempts to promote contentment on the farm.[6]

To country life publicists, the unceasing drift to the city was the major symptom of the decline of rural civilization. As such, it provided them with the chief basis for their many proposals to ameliorate conditions of farm life, for they reasoned that if country living were more attractive people would stay on the farm. This is what was implied when reformers spoke of developing a rural existence that was "satisfying and worthy of the best desires" of country dwellers.[7]

Some writers maintained that migration to the city had the insidious result of removing the "best" spirits, the most capable and vigorous people, from the rural population. The less fit, they argued, stayed in the country to reproduce at a higher rate than city people, which contributed to genetic deterioration of the nation and possible "race suicide." If the exodus from the country continued, America would suffer in the future from worn-out soil, an inadequate food supply, and a biologically inferior civilization. The implicit racism of these writers seems to have been a concomitant of the thinking of numerous country life reformers, as well as a part of the thought of the times. A major concern of rural reformers seems to have been to preserve native-born people on the land as moral mainstays, for America could not depend upon "the pauperized villages of Europe, the deserts of Asia, and the jungles of Africa" for people to ripen and perfect her civilization.[8]

The assumption that rural migration always took the best youths of a community was investigated seriously by sociologists of a later era. Carle C. Zimmerman and Wilson Gee made a series of investigations of the migration phenomenon in the 1920s, but came up with conflicting and inconclusive results. Using educational attainment to indicate the more promising members in the rural community, they took samples in a number of farming communities in the Midwest and East Coast areas. Gee's studies tended to support the thesis that the more able moved to the cities, while Zimmerman concluded that rural migration was largely a matter of the most promising and least promising leaving the country, with the solid, middle farming elements remaining on the land.[9]

The flight to the city also raised the question as to whether or not fewer farmers could feed the rapidly growing general population. Expanding medical knowledge and the use of better sanitation methods were causing the death rate to decline more rapidly than the birth rate, and some people feared that farmers would be unable to meet the food demands of the increasing millions. This, combined with the belief that the nation's supply of tillable land was exhausted, caused great alarm among the consuming public. Irrigation of land in the West and intensive farming were put forward as ways to delay the eventuality of the population outstripping food production, but they were admittedly expensive and required labor at a time it was leaving the countryside. Frightening as the prospect seemed, the crucial factor overlooked by those who used these neo-Malthusian arguments, as well as those who responded to them, was that the rate of population increase was declining although the population itself was growing. Moreover, the potentialities of the application of scientific agricultural techniques were something no one could accurately gauge. Some reformers did, of course, note the higher yields of farms where improved cultivation methods were used and they were reassured by the possibilities that could come from increased use of fertilizers, farm machinery, and land conservation.[10]

Certain urban elements saw the solution to the rural-to-urban problem in terms of relocating city residents in the country, and they tried to persuade people to move to the land by stressing the joys of rural living and the ease of working a small, intensively cultivated farm. This "back-to-the-land" movement had at least three discernible sources. There was, first of all, the city dwellers' fear, already discussed, that the declining farm population would not be able to feed them. Rising prices of foodstuffs, declining exports, and the high cost of living duly enforced this belief. Secondly, there was the urban concern with congestion and the negative effects of overpopulation on the quality of city life. Humanitarians and social workers, in particular, were appalled by the big city slums and actively sought to settle newly arrived immigrants on the land, sometimes even promoting agricultural colonies made up of the newcomers. Others, fearful of what might happen to the city if internal and external migration continued unabated, less nobly supported efforts to send people to uncrowded rural districts.[11] A third source was the reaction of many individuals to the highly structured, institutionalized society associated with industrialism, which expressed itself in a primitivistic desire to go back to nature and simplicity. There were back-to-the-land movements in a number of industrialized nations during this period, and they also seemed to be part of a phenomenon related to advancing industrialism and urbanization. Apparently many people were frustrated and dissatisfied in the face of the vast and complex changes brought by industrialism and they yearned for simpler times and all the imagined goodness which they associated with them.[12]

However, not everyone in the country life movement was convinced that settling urbanites on the land promised a solution to the rural problem. Some, in fact, staunchly opposed any indiscriminate dumping of city people, many of whom were described as "undesirable," onto the country. At its hearings, the Country Life Commission found that farmers voiced this same feeling, some even stating that the problems resulting from the sending of the city poor into rural areas were so bad as to create the need for a mounted police force in country districts. Another back-to-the-land type whom some reformers would not encourage was the wealthy man who wanted a country estate on which to dabble in agriculture. Such people, it was argued, would live in the country but they would never really be a part of it.[13]

Liberty Hyde Bailey and other reformers did not object to qualified individuals being sent to the farm. Indeed, Bailey even suggested that there should be agencies in large cities which could give information to those genuinely interested in farming, and Walter Hines Page published articles in his *World's Work* magazine devoted to purchasing a farm, farming costs, and other matters related to entering farming. Most country life workers were cautious, however, in their endorsement of back-to-the-land efforts. They tended to agree with the viewpoint of Thomas Nixon Carver, a Harvard economist, that the real purpose of the country life movement was not to attempt to colonize people on the farms but to stem the tide of migration to the city by finding and removing, if possible, the causes for people leaving the farms.[14]

The back-to-the-land movement failed, except for some of the colonizing attempts, especially those involving Jewish and other immigrants, and a few wealthy people who bought farms to use as weekend and summer homes.[15] The meager results point up the effort's lack of an economic foundation. If a real need for more men on the land had existed, farm prices and wages should have risen, but they did so only slightly and even then were always below the average for all commodities and labor. Instead of agriculture needing more manpower, it apparently needed less.

Farming in the narrow sense of the practices of those who tilled the soil received a great deal of attention from reformers because it seemed to many of them to be the chief means for bettering the farmers' lot and improving their status. They reasoned that if people left farming because it held no promise of success, then it should be made successful. Many of the "problems" of farming in that day were caused by the impact of industrialism upon agriculture and the economy, and many country life reformers correctly concluded that farmers needed to use more scientific techniques, be more efficient, and become businessmen. In this way agriculture would be economically successful, able to keep pace with the rest of the economy, and capable of supplying more food with a smaller number in the farm population.

An observable phenomenon of agriculture in transition during the early years of the century was the so-called "abandoned farm" seen so commonly in the East and written about so often in the literature of the time. Most of these abandoned farms were merely vacant farm buildings, for the land was still being tilled but by someone who had bought out the previous owner.[16] The tendency was toward a rationalization of agriculture through the use of farms which would give optimum efficiency, and the so-called "abandoned farm" generally represented this reassembling of agricultural business units. Despite his romantic agrarianism, Bailey was one of the few in the country life movement who seemed to recognize this fact, and he exposed the incongruous position of those who prophesied great changes for agriculture but who insisted, out of sentiment, on the same accidental division of fifty years earlier, the eighty-acre farm.[17] Like Janus, they were looking in two directions at the same time; indeed, their position manifested the major dilemma of the country life movement.

Farm units were not the only feature of agriculture undergoing change, for the tenure arrangement in agriculture was also shifting. Since Jefferson's time the American tradition had stressed the small family-owned farm, but by 1900 tenancy and absentee landlordism had increased to the place where over one-third of the farms in the country were operated by tenants. Moreover, figures released by the Census Bureau in 1914 indicated that fifty-two percent of the farmers in the United States moved from their farms in less than five years time, reflecting the geographic mobility and rootlessness associated with tenancy. Because of the sentimental attachment to the independent, landowning husbandman as an ideal type, these statistics were disturbing to many people. Theodore Roosevelt probably expressed the feelings of countless fellow citizens when he stated that no one wanted to see American farmers reduced to the level of European peasants, who barely made a living on their small holdings. Ironically, something similar to that condition was even then working itself out for some farmers. Today, the tendency is nearly complete, with one portion of the rural population virtually proletarianized and the other, smaller, but more dominant group, coming increasingly to identify itself and its interests with the urban middle class.[18]

Not only were tenancy and absentee ownership increasing near the turn of the century, there were also indications that the "agricultural ladder," or mobility pattern in agriculture, was becoming less functional.[19] Rising successively from hired hand to tenant to owner was still possible, but the stages were growing increasingly farther apart, making it more difficult to move from one to another. An important part of the explanation for this was the rapidly rising cost of land, which caused potential farm owners to spend longer lengths of time in the status of hired hands and tenants. To remedy the situation, some reformers urged that governmental assistance be given to young men who wished to acquire farms. In addition, reformers proposed that the conditions of farm labor be improved so that workers would not be driven from farming by unnecessary discouragement.[20]

Tenancy was mainly an economic problem but it did have certain social side effects which greatly distressed country life reformers. They contended, for example, that roads, schools, churches, and community life in general suffered when farm owners moved to town and were replaced by renters. This was so, they declared, because absentee owners were generally opposed to taxation for school and road improvements, withdrew their financial support from the country church, which reduced its effectiveness, and ceased their civic-minded participation in rural community life. The tenants who supplanted them, on the other hand, usually considered themselves transients and were likewise unconcerned about these matters. Moreover, the custom of leasing farms on a yearly basis destroyed the tenants' incentive to keep up the physical appearance of the farms they rented, since they usually would not invest in anything which they might leave shortly and gratuitously to their successors or to the owners. As an obvious solution to this problem, reformers urged that the length of farm leases be extended so that tenants might recover their investment on improvements.[21]

There is reason to believe that these complaints contained much that was valid, but the real source of the difficulty would seem to have been the landlords, who in many instances were speculators waiting for the buyer who would pay the right price. If that were generally true, then the solution of the tenancy issue actually awaited the resolution of the speculation problem, which was largely an outgrowth of the farmers' acceptance of the acquisitive goals and speculative temper of business society.[22] Few country life reformers seemed to recognize, however, that in urging the farmer to become businesslike they were bringing about the destruction of those values associated with his yeoman past which they most treasured. It was as if they imagined seriously that they could have the best of both worlds.

The latent racism of the early twentieth-century crusaders for rural betterment, noted earlier, expressed itself most pronouncedly with respect to the tenancy issue. Reformers declared that many of those who came as tenants were not desirable additions to the community because of their foreign origins and ways. Less overt, but as reflective of an intolerant and chauvinistic attitude, were the repeated expressions of distress over the declining number of native Americans in the farm population and the implicit peril this fact held for the nation from the reformers' viewpoint. Typical of this kind of covert racism was William S. Rossiter's statement that the declining farm population was being replaced by "foreigners" who might be useful to the nation someday, but at the time they were not "in harmony with the spirit of the institutions created by the native stock."[23]

In parts of the country the increase in tenancy was directly related to the shortage of labor, one of the deficiencies most complained of during this period. The difficulty of securing labor was so great, reformers maintained, that some farmers were driven to dispose of their farms or to rent them to tenants. Agriculture's labor shortage was real, but it was due chiefly to its inability to compete effectively with urban enterprise, which in turn was related to the transition it was undergoing. Farmers had not yet made farming a business to the point where they could hire men all year around at wages comparable to those paid in the city. Of course, there were other handicaps such as the long hours, tedious work, and lack of conveniences and comforts which farmers would need to overcome before they could attract labor as easily as urban employers.[24]

Some country life reformers saw the increased use of machinery that would eliminate the need for additional workers as the answer to the farmers' labor problem. Others believed intensive farming, wherein high cash crops were cultivated on a reduced acreage, was a viable solution since it required little extra help but allowed farmers to earn as much as they did through extensive cultivation. One reform publicist reasoned that the "little-farm-well-tilled" would even help to increase the rural population by allowing more people to live on the land, since a three-hundred-acre farm could then be subdivided into a half dozen fifty-acre farmsteads! To say the least, this would reverse the trend toward consolidation of agricultural units, which Bailey and some others recognized was taking place. Moreover, those who proposed that farmers increase the mechanization or specialization of their enterprise overlooked the fact that both of these required skilled workers, who were not common to agriculture at the time.[25]

Still other reformers insisted that the only real solution to the farm labor problem lay in improved methods of agriculture that would enable farmers to employ their hired men by the year. Occasionally, someone even suggested that farmers ought to rely more heavily on immigrant labor but, as noted above, resentment of immigrants in agriculture was more common among reformers. One of the more unique reform recommendations was that local industries be established in the country so that farmers could use workers seasonally and the factories could employ them during the rest of the year.[26]

Of all the features of agriculture which demanded change, according to the rural reformers' analysis, the one most symbolic of its inferior status was its low economic reward when compared to other occupations. Per capita income of farmers always lagged behind that of urban occupations, and the charge was frequently made that people deserted the land because farming did not pay enough. Some reformers carried the argument to great lengths, one declaring that farmers long ago would have fallen to the condition of peasants were it not for specialization, a certain amount of scientific farming, and the vast acres of virgin soil of the past. Another held that farmers only made a living by using their wives and children as laborers, so close was the margin between profit and loss.[27] Charges such as these imply economic discontent, yet paradoxically, they were made during a time of general agricultural prosperity which most people recognized.

Much of the concern reflected in these statements was probably for the farmers' lost status as much as for genuine economic distress among agriculturists. Arguments that farmers were "disadvantaged," or the victims of "marked inequalities," or "not receiving the full rewards" to which they were entitled run through the writings of country life reformers.[28] They were equivalent to saying that farmers did not have equality of opportunity, which was the means of social mobility, in American society. The farmers' position was down and there it would stay unless something were done to raise it.

While many thought the way to solve this problem was to make farming more profitable and worked in that direction, a division in country life thinking caused others to challenge the idea as a real solution.[29] Mabel Carney, a normal school professor, declared that economic satisfaction was not enough—if it were, then why were so many country people still migrating to the city in the Midwest, where farmers were prosperous? It seemed to her that more was needed. Life in the country, she reasoned, had to be made attractive both spiritually and ideally as well as economically and socially. But how was this to be done? Carney and others in the movement believed it would come through proper education, which would reveal and promote this other side of farm life.[30]

A matter which was definitely related to the farmers' margin of profit was the market situation. Today it is in the nature of a truism to note that with the change to commercial farming, agriculturists became dependent upon world market and economic conditions and that they could no longer ignore distribution as an important part of their concern. But during the first decades of the century this fact was not commonplace among farmers, nor was it grasped by all country life reformers. Many city people, however, did relate the rising cost of living to profits of the middleman, and they reasoned that if these were reduced, or if the middleman were eliminated entirely, both consumers and farmers would benefit. Obviously there is an element of self-interest in such urban support of better marketing for farmers, but many country life reformers viewed the effort as one aimed chiefly at increasing the farmers' profits as part of the program to raise their standing as progressive businessmen who operated efficient enterprises.

Some reformers thought the federal government should aid farmers with their marketing problems. Therefore, when the Country Life Commission urged in 1909 that the government undertake a study of business practices affecting farmers, they particularly recommended an investigation of the handling of farm products. Partly as a result of that recommendation, and partly through the efforts of farm organizations such as the Farmers' Union, an Office of Markets was established within the Department of Agriculture in 1913. The new agency gave farmers an increasing amount of information and guidance relating to the distribution of their products until the 1920s when it was merged with the Office of Farm Management and made the Bureau of Agricultural Economics.[31]

Cooperative organization was the remedy which reformers most often suggested to solve the farmers' marketing problem. Concentration of control in industry seemed to account for the ability of manufacturers to maintain the prices of their products, and reformers urged farmers to attain the same control through cooperation since they could not accomplish it individually. Here the new farm organizations took the lead and thousands of cooperative enterprises were established during the first quarter of the twentieth century.[32] These were specialized business ventures, usually organized on a local basis. Like the Grange stores of the 1870s, most were formed along lines of the Rochdale Plan, with one vote per man, a limited return on the capital invested, and the distribution of surplus income in accordance with each man's share in the business. Farm organizations, however, did not conceive of cooperation in quite the same way urban consumers did.

To the former, it was essentially a matter of farmer concern, while to the latter it was a matter of joint activity.[33]

Easier credit was considered by reformers as another means for bettering the farmers' welfare by putting more money in their pockets. This was not a new idea, for most of the farm movements of the late nineteenth century had advocated it, as indeed they had proposed many of the ideas put forth by country life reformers. The need for better agricultural credit was apparent, since the rising cost of land and the increased use of machinery, fertilizers, better seeds, and improved livestock required greater outlays of capital over longer periods of time, and the existing banking system failed to provide the credit. Furthermore, it was rather unrealistic to persuade farmers to adopt commercial business practices and not urge the creation of adequate credit facilities at the same time.

Much urban support of rural credit proposals is therefore understandable in terms of the effort to convert the farmer into a businessman. However, the awareness of city dwellers that there were thousands of acres of land lying idle in the West because people lacked the capital necessary to open them through irrigation and dry farming was no doubt another important reason. The psychological effects this realization had upon people who were alarmed at the decreasing farm population and fearful of a food shortage can be easily understood. If more land were put into production, they might reason, supply would catch up to demand, the cost of living would go down, and peace of mind plus pocketbooks would be restored.[34]

The remedy for the farmers' credit problem which reformers most often proposed was the joint-stock bank, although a number of other cooperative credit schemes were put forth as solutions during the period. One reformer actually thought the whole problem of farmer credit could be solved if loans were made to farmers on the basis of their character. This was not really as absurd as it sounded, for, as the author of the idea pointed out, bankers in rural communities ought to know farmers well enough to judge their ability to repay. More importantly, bankers would investigate all requests for loans to determine whether or not the money would be used in a productive enterprise. This, he argued, would be beneficial all around in that it would get the banker out of his office and into the country where he could become acquainted with the real nature of the farmers' problems.[35]

After years of discussion, the federal government finally established, underwrote, and operated a system of long-term credit. When first introduced in 1914, the rural credit measure was blocked by President Wilson and Secretary of Agriculture Houston; however, it won full support of the administration in 1916, when farm votes were needed by the Democrats in order to carry the presidential election of that year. Enacted into law as the Federal Farm Loan Act, it provided for twelve farm land banks with an initial capitalization of $500,000 each and for forty-year loans at six percent interest. Some condemned the law for not going far enough, while others castigated it as a dangerous socialistic scheme which used the money of all the people to provide loans for farmers at rates of interest below those available to others. Still, the legislation seemed popular, for it passed almost unanimously in both houses of Congress, 58 to 5 in the Senate and 295 to 10 in the House.[36]

Another financial measure primarily for farmers, and one pressed to adoption during Taft's administration, was the postal savings bank system. Reformers maintained that farmers did not have adequate savings facilities and those that existed were not regulated to provide for the safety of deposits, which tended therefore to discourage thrift among the men on the land. A postal saving system, they believed, would provide a safe place for the small savings of rural people and also strengthen thrift, which was weakening as a rural value. It made sense, moreover, to utilize the postal system for this purpose since there was a post office in nearly every hamlet in the nation. As might be expected, however, there was some opposition to the legislation from country bankers, who saw the system as competition and a threat to their enterprises.[37]

Reformers demanded still more postal services for country people in the form of a parcel post system. Legislation was enacted in 1912, but not without a struggle with the transportation companies and small town merchants, both of whom feared the government's threat to their profits and security. The law's relationship to the broad effort to make rural life pleasing is obvious, for many farmers were in a position during these years to support the gaudiest dreams of mail-order houses if only the merchandise could be delivered conveniently and without great expense. It is also apparent that parcel post legislation conferred substantial advantages upon the mail-order firms by enabling them to overcome a serious barrier to their future growth. Just as clearly, the agricultural aid, farm shows, and contests sponsored by catalogue firms such as Sears, Roebuck and Company emanated from this awareness that the success of their enterprises had a crucial reference to rural welfare and development.[38]

But of the many aspects of the rural problem which caused concern among reformers, the lack of good roads was one of the most frequently discussed. In the minds of many Americans, urban and rural residents alike, the condition of the nation's country thoroughfares was a national disgrace. Significantly, the Country Life Commission during its investigation in 1908 found it to be one of the two most often mentioned needs of rural people. It was so important, reformers maintained, because inadequate roads were directly related to many other problems. Bad roads, for example, contributed to the isolation and loneliness of farm life, to the decadence of the rural school and church, to the farmers' marketing problems, to lowered land values, and to the rural exodus.[39]

Interestingly, good roads sentiment was awakened in the 1890s by urban bicycle enthusiasts who demanded better roads on which to pedal out into the country. During that same period rural free delivery became a reality for farm folk and there was added the interest in better roads on the part of the federal government and some of the farm people themselves. Then in the early twentieth century the automobile came into wider use and good roads agitation picked up momentum, especially as significant numbers of farmers acquired the new vehicles. The leading good roads promoters, however, were urban interests, such as bicycle and road machinery groups, railroads which saw improved rural arteries as feeders for their lines, and academicians who were concerned about more efficient highway administration. It was only as farmers became more market-conscious during the early years of the century that the relationship of better roads to transportation costs was brought home to them in such a way as to elicit their support and enthusiasm.[40]

Part of the road problem was the confused situation with respect to responsibility and control. As of 1912 only half the states in the Union had anything approaching centralized control.

In some states, roads were the responsibility of the county supervisors, in others they were under township control, and in still
others they were entrusted to a combination of state, county, and
township control. With such a varied situation, reformers had
little trouble demonstrating waste due to mismanagement and
partisan politics. They proposed therefore that highway construction, control, and maintenance be taken out of politics and that
more attention be given to scientific road management. However, the essential cautiousness of rural reform leaders kept most
of them from advocating federally financed road programs and
so therefore they supported the milder proposal that the national
government supply engineering services to the states.[41]

Some of the special road organizations which were most
active in the effort to improve country highways and byways were
the National Good Roads Association established in 1900, the
American Association for Highway Improvement formed in
1910, and the Farmers' Good Roads League. All of these held
conferences and disseminated information concerning ways to
improve rural roads. During the period two special road magazines, *Good Roads* and *Southern Good Roads,* were started and
helped awaken public sentiment with respect to country roads.
Other groups, agencies, and developments which were part of the
reform milieu and helped stimulate interest in the public highways during the years near the turn of the century were road
equipment concerns, road improvement conferences, the Office
of Good Roads, "good roads" trains, and the movement to con-
solidate country schools. In addition, there were groups too numerous to mention which in one way or another had an indirect
interest or involvement in road improvements.[42]

The relationship between good roads and the efforts of reformers to make rural life more satisfying is quite evident. Theodore Roosevelt and other country life leaders saw good roads as
one of the primary ways to relieve rural isolation and to stem the
tide of migration to the cities. Ironically, the very roads meant
to ease the farmers' loneliness provided them with a means to
come into even greater contact with urban society, which had the
effect of speeding up the alteration of rural habits, institutions,
and traditional ideas. The dilemma of country life reformers is
once more apparent, for in leading farmers into the twentieth

century, the agrarian ideals which made them the objects of so much concern were profoundly changed.

* * *

With the possible exception of the rural exodus, the discussion by reformers of the foregoing problems pales almost to unimportance when compared to the outpourings concerned with rural education. It was cited as the cause for dissatisfaction and people leaving the countryside more often than anything else. The principal complaint was that the rural school educated country youths away from the land by stimulating their imaginations with the adventure and variety of city experience and by generally preparing them for urban life. Teachers were accused of being urban-oriented and of encouraging farm children to think of choosing other occupations, while the curriculum in the country school was reproached for stressing preparation for nonfarming careers. Even textbooks were indicted for using urban examples, phrasing problems in terms of things common to city life, and in general utilizing terms and materials foreign to the experiences and day-to-day living of farm youngsters. Moreover, in educating farm youth away from the land, the rural school was neglecting its *raison d'être,* namely, to prepare people for country life. The school was therefore held responsible for causing young people to migrate to the cities and for the poor farming done by those who stayed behind on the farms. The reformers' demand was for a school that would change this situation by teaching love of country life and giving practical training in agriculture.[43]

As rural reformers continued to attack the country school for its ineffectiveness, professional educators joined the movement and spoke out against other deficiencies. The rural school was stagnant and wasteful, they argued, because it had too few students to provide for an efficient utilization of instructional facilities. Educational authorities reported in 1908, for example, that there were two states in the Midwest which together had nearly four hundred schools with less than five pupils enrolled![44] Often this situation was due to the harmful practice of dividing and subdividing districts so that ambitious farmers had a schoolhouse near their farmyards as an imagined benefit for their own offspring. Educators charged further that country schools had poorly trained teachers and shabbily constructed, ill-ventilated, ill-heated, and generally unhealthy buildings. Moreover, the school year was too short, being only three or four months in some instances, and the period of formal instruction was equally brief, lasting only five or six years in many places.[45]

Some critics of the rural school complained that its teachers and administrators were either incompetent or people who looked upon their positions in the country school as an apprenticeship for eventual placement in a city system. As the president of a state normal school cleverly commented, the typical rural teacher looked upon the country school as "a little house on a little ground with a little equipment where a little teacher at a little salary for a little while taught little children little things."[46] Reformers believed, furthermore, that most rural teachers were ill-equipped for country life leadership both by training and predisposition since they were unprepared to teach agriculture or the sciences on which it rested and they possessed no abiding sympathy for rural life. Charges of incompetency were also leveled at school board officials, common complaints being that they were untrained, lacking in vision, and often self-interested.[47]

To many reformers, the principal remedy of the rural school problem was to redirect it in such a way that it would prepare young people for rural living. The method most often proposed to accomplish this was based on the philosophy of Liberty Hyde Bailey and John Dewey and involved relating the school to its environment. Specifically, it meant introducing nature study into the school curriculum, and school gardens were commonly put forward as a way to give pupils close contact with nature, although a nature orientation was to pervade all course work and thus promote the idealization of country life. In a similar manner, the school should be related to community life by teaching subjects in familiar farming terms, such as those suggested by Liberty Hyde Bailey and noted earlier in this study. Even textbooks used by country children should be changed to reflect the farm and nature orientation.[48]

According to country life reformers, the redirected school should also teach scientific agriculture and other practical subjects. It was recommended, however, that agricultural science be taught at the high school level, where students could more readily grasp its principles and become aware of the profit, both monetary and spiritual, of intelligent and efficient farming.

Home economics, manual training, and health and sanitation principles were also proposed by reformers as valuable supplementary subjects to be taught in the new rural school.[49]

Reformers urged, furthermore, that something be done about the preparation of rural teachers. "Our normal schools must send us persons trained to a delicate and intimate acquaintance with nature," one reformer declared.[50] Inspired themselves, he stated, such teachers would inspire their pupils. However, to get this sort of teacher required a different preparation than the one prospective teachers were then receiving. Nature study and agricultural principles would have to be taught in teacher training institutions and for those already teaching, summer sessions would need to be utilized to give them such training. But in addition to a better education for rural teachers, reformers also demanded a complete reorganization of the school working staff of administrators, supervisors, and teachers.[51]

In the end, it was an awesome task which reformers set for the rural teacher. Not only did she need to teach the fundamentals well, but she also had to give good instruction in gardening, manual training, sewing, and cooking. Moreover, she was expected to inspire farm children with such a love for the country that they would not want to leave it and she was also to improve the school in terms of its physical equipment, sanitation, decorations, and recreational facilities. In addition, she was counted upon to encourage farmers to do better farming and their wives to be better homemakers. With such an assignment, one wonders that teachers stayed in country schools as long as they did! However, the reality of the situation was that no teacher could do all the things country life reformers would have her do, but dedicated teachers could, and did, attempt to do many of them.

The consolidated school was looked upon by most rural reformers as "the best solution of the country school problem yet devised."[52] Their view was supported by studies of experimentally combined schools which showed that these new schools were superior to one-room schools both in long-term economy and social and educational benefits. Furthermore, they were endorsed by ninety-five percent of the farmers who gave them a fair trial. Especially important from the reformers' viewpoint were the possibilities for agricultural education promised by consolidation, since the larger facilities would provide laboratories and land to use for experiments and demonstrations. The greater wealth of an enlarged school district would also permit payment of the better salaries necessary to recruit teachers who were properly trained to teach agricultural subjects. In addition, many reformers believed the consolidated school would build up a sense of community better than numerous separate units since it would provide more facilities and incentives to draw the surrounding population together.[53]

Country life reformers saw both discouragement and hopefulness in the rural school situation. On the one hand, country schools exhibited the effects of their isolation from the mainstream of educational reform taking place during the nineteenth century. But on the other hand, they promised a resolution of the rural problem through a transformation which would cause them to promote effective farming, rural idealism, and satisfaction with country life.

*   *   *

Deterioration of the country church, the other major rural institution, was another aspect of the rural problem which received widespread attention from reform elements during the years near the turn of the century. Reformers were particularly disturbed by the failure of the church to promote community ideals, which they considered the great spiritual need of the rural population at that time. The country church, they said, still clung to a narrow emphasis on doctrine and an outworn orthodoxy which made no real link between religion and the social problems of the day. Its diminishing congregations, poorly-paid ministers, and dilapidated and abandoned buildings were symptoms of its decline and its failure to adapt to the modern age.[54]

Sectarian emphasis on doctrinal distinctions, reformers believed, was to blame for much of the church's ineffectiveness, because it kept three or four churches in a community struggling to preserve their separate identities when the number of active churchgoers would justify adequate support of only one. In view of declining membership and financial support, insistence on these divisions seemed ridiculous to many people. Some advocates of country church reform suspected, however, that it was not always doctrinal differences and ethnic origins which separated groups, but that it was often "grudges, resentments, and narrow and mean social feelings."[55]

Reformers also blamed the rural pastorate for the church's degeneration. Some indicted country ministers for being intolerant toward change, especially towards the new amusements of young people such as Saturday night dances and Sunday baseball games. Others charged that many rural ministers, like some country school teachers, were merely putting in their time in the country church while waiting for a call to a city pulpit. Still others accused rural clergymen of placing denominational interests before those of the community and of cutting themselves off from the social life of the country. Indeed, some rural ministers actually lived in the city, which caused physical removal from their flocks as well as intellectual and social isolation. Furthermore, the shortage of rural ministers meant that some pastors were responsible for several churches and this generally meant that they had no close ties with any of their congregations.[56]

Some who assessed the rural church situation saw the church's decline as an economic problem at bottom. The deterioration of the church, they argued, was deep-rooted in the economic changes of the first decade of the new century, when high land values caused a shifting of population in the country, with the resulting breakdown in community spirit and pride. The church had failed to come up with a new program attacking this problem and was paying the price in terms of decay. Until the church recognized that economic ills required economic remedies rather than theological ones, these analysts insisted, there would be no salvation for the country church.[57]

Most supporters of rural church betterment believed that the real solution to the church problem was to have churches and ministers recognize their new social mission and thereby fulfill their responsibilities to the rural community. Rural clergymen should be taught to idealize country life, even to the point of making *it* a religion. They should do less preaching about Jesus and more practicing of what he did. Parishioners, on the other hand, should be made to understand that the most powerful religious feeling finds expression in unselfish living and social service rather than in concern with theological discussions. They should realize, furthermore, that civic rightness and right-

eousness were the same thing. Too often in the past, many reformers contended, righteousness had been associated with another existence whereas it was actually realizable here in this
life through honesty, uprightness, and civic duty.[58]

Some supporters of country church revitalization even suggested that ministers be given agricultural courses during their
seminary training so that they might be abreast of those in the
rural world where they would work. These enthusiasts would
have pastors spreading information on scientific agriculture,
holding institutes and demonstrations, organizing marketing
cooperatives, and generally stimulating their congregations to
do more effective farming. Not everyone agreed with this idea,
however.[59] As Warren Wilson, Superintendent of the Department of Church and Country Life of the Presbyterian Church
stated with a note of barbed humor, "the modern minister is
to serve not vegetables, but men."[60] Because the minister worked
with human beings living in society, he continued, he should be
a specialist in social science and not the soil sciences or animal
husbandry. In the end, it was this latter viewpoint which carried
the day, for by 1915 several theological seminaries did add rural
sociology courses to their regular curriculum.

Federation was the remedy reformers most commonly
offered to strengthen the country church in the local community.
Unified churches would bring together into one thriving church
the members of several smaller, dying congregations. Since people of all denominations would be represented in these community churches, doctrinal differences could be ignored and
leadership in social service activity would be asserted. The re-
vitalized and strengthened church would then be able to provide
the spiritual, social, and economic direction needed by the rural
community.[61]

*   *   *

It seems improbable that rural conditions were as inadequate as country life reformers described them, since the period
was one of general farm prosperity. Undoubtedly many of the
conditions described did exist, but only in certain areas and they
could hardly be applied to agriculture in general. If circumstances were as serious as the reformers' analysis would indicate,
there should have been an upwelling of farmer dissatisfaction,
but there was not. Actually, the greatest discontent during the

period seems to have existed among rural reformers rather than among farmers.

Moreover, many of the proposals which reformers offered for the improvement of rural life seem unrealistic. For example, farmers probably were not very enthusiastic over suggestions that they be less materialistic and play more often. Understandably concerned about the economic aspects of their enterprises, they would most likely have appreciated more practical advice which would have increased their income. Other proposals were unrealistic because they exceeded the ability of most farmers to achieve them even if they would have desired to do so. The money required, for instance, to renovate one's farmstead, afford new machinery and methods of agriculture, and support a better school presumed a standard of living which was probably well above that of the average farmer, even during prosperous times.

In considering these matters, it must be remembered that rural life reformers had little real contact with agriculture. They were not farmers, and even those who were farm-reared had lived in cities for years and were largely urban in their outlook. Such people were not close to the monotony of chores, the dust of harrowing and threshing, the threat of drought and insect pests, and other disagreeable aspects of rural existence. The view of farm life held by most of these people was the rose-colored one found in literature or recalled through the mists of childhood memories. Their lives were lived in urban comfort, and it was quite easy for them to idealize country life. They therefore failed to realize that for countless numbers life on the farm was not a satisfying existence in a society which was becoming rapidly urbanized and affluent. Nor did they seem to recognize that no amount of improvement of country life could keep people on the land when conditions set in motion by industrialization were forcing them to leave.

chapter six

Techniques of Country Life Reform

 ᴊnere were essentially five methods, if they may be called
that, which were adopted by reformers to promote rural improvement: surveys, educational extension work, conferences, publicity,
and legislation. Those in the country life movement considered all
five important to the advancement of rural reconstruction, although they did not necessarily place the same emphasis on each
of them. Consistent with their belief that ultimately country
people themselves had to resolve rural problems, reformers
stressed that these methods were intended only to disseminate
knowledge, provide guidance, remove handicaps, and stimulate
the farm population to develop a better rural civilization.

 Ac ording to reformers, surveys were the first step in the
creation of a scientifically and economically sound country life,
because the information gathered was needed to determine the
extent of problems and to draw up prescriptions for their resolution. Bailey used the method in his horticultural work as early as
1896, but one of the first uses of it as an instrument for social
investigation was a study of Tompkins County, New York, begun
in 1906 by George F. Warren and others at Cornell University.
As applied to rural problems, the survey involved a vast inventory
of soil and climatic conditions, farming methods, the market and
labor situation, roads, schools, churches, social life, and all the
advantages and disadvantages of a given locality. The Country
Life Commission stated in its report in 1909 that the survey

method was fundamental to the program of rural betterment and recommended a massive and detailed investigation of all agricultural and country life conditions. After that a great many surveys were made, so many in fact that one observer was led to remark that " we are living in an age of surveys."[1]

Among the first to take up the method were religious groups seeking information which might help reestablish the influence of the church in rural areas. Of these early studies, those conducted by Warren H. Wilson of the Home Missions Board of the Presbyterian Church were particularly important in terms of the information gathered. Wilson had become interested in the survey method while doing graduate work at Columbia with Professor Franklin H. Giddings, a pioneer in the use of surveys in social research. Subsequently, Wilson made a sociological study of a church community as his doctoral dissertation, which was published as the first of a number of rural church surveys he conducted. Gifford Pinchot, demonstrating the variety of his far-ranging interests, worked with clergyman Charles O. Gill on another important survey of the country church situation, which was also published. Gill became very interested in survey work and was later involved in a massive survey of the rural church throughout the state of Ohio.[2]

At the college and university level, surveys gave an impetus to the growth of rural sociology and to its acceptance as a discipline in the college curriculum. In fact, most of the social surveys sponsored by institutions of higher learning during the period were conducted by rural sociologists. Interested in rural social relations and their improvement, these academicians collected much data, which they published in the hope of stimulating farmer interest in a better country life. The work of these pioneering sociologists has endured as one of the accomplishments of the country life movement, and the new discipline they brought into being continues to perpetuate interest in rural life matters although the great concern generated near the turn of the century has subsided.[3]

Country school personnel who were part of the rural reform effort also adopted the survey method as a device to promote school and community improvement. Teachers often directed their pupils to collect information about the community, which was then published in the local newspapers to encourage rural people to improve their neighborhoods. As professional educators became interested in the rural problem, they also discussed the possibilities of surveys for revealing inadequacies of both school systems and agricultural communities. Sometimes these surveys revealed rather shocking facts about the school situation, as did the one in Whitley County, Kentucky, where is was discovered that only sixty-three percent of the children of school age attended classes and that only one school in six had even a single pupil complete the elementary course. In 1913, the National Council of Education set up a Committee on School Efficiency to encourage and aid in the making of school surveys throughout the nation. Throughout the period of this study, educational journals increasingly devoted articles to the subject of surveys and textbooks on rural education began adding sections on the method.[4]

Certainly it would be rather easy to underestimate the value of the survey to farm life reform efforts since the giant investigation of all facets of the rural problem called for by the County Life Commission was never made. Enough studies were undertaken, however, to demonstrate the worth of the method, and by their work with the survey rural reformers and others left little doubt that the systematic gathering of facts provided a scientific approach to problem solving and sound planning. This, in the end, was the real significance of the survey.

                              *   *   *

Important as surveys were as a device for bringing about country life improvement, they were not nearly as significant as educational extension work in the thinking of reformers. As was pointed out earlier in this study, belief in the efficacy of education, especially of agricultural education, was an article of faith for most rural life reformers. Convinced that the majority of farmers were not using scientific practices to improve their lot, reformers supported extension teaching as the most effective means to eliminate rural ignorance and indifference. Moreover, they firmly believed that this kind of educational work would increase agricultural efficiency, profits, and the possibilities of country life.[5]

While reformers had no doubt as to the effectiveness of extension education, there was some question at first as to the specific form it should take. Both the agricultural colleges and the United States Department of Agriculture were engaged in such work, but each had a different approach. Whereas the land grant schools used primarily exhibits, farmers' institutes, and a variety of publications, the Department of Agriculture utilized cooperative demonstration methods which employed selected farmers as "demonstrators."[6]

From the outset, however, the cooperative demonstration work of the Department of Agriculture seemed to produce better results than the efforts of the agricultural colleges and the experiment stations associated with them. Seaman A. Knapp began the work at Terrell, Texas, in 1903, and within a decade its popularity had spread throughout the nation. Although the Department of Agriculture endorsed the work, actual financial support for it came from businessmen who had a stake in the farmers' welfare and therefore looked upon demonstration work as a way to promote agricultural efficiency and prosperity. In 1906 the Rockefeller General Education Board began to sponsor the work, thereby giving it a highly respectable stamp of approval. Soon business interests and chambers of commerce outside the South were stimulated to support the work, and the system became nationwide.[7]

By 1914 the land grant colleges and the Department of Agriculture alike were using the demonstration method, which had become so popular that both were seeking federal funds to support their work. In that year the Smith-Lever Act combined the two educational activities by having the agricultural colleges, subject to approval by the Department of Agriculture, advise all extension agents. Financially, the work was to be supported by federal, state, local, and even private moneys.[8]

Before the events of 1914 resulted in the consolidation of the extension work, both approaches gave attention to the social aspects of country life as well as to the technical side of farming. The institutes held by the agricultural colleges, for example, discussed the need for household conveniences as well as the problems of cooperative economic organization. The promotion of women's institutes and boys' and girls' farm clubs was a further manifestation of the importance the college extension program placed on the social needs of the agricultural community. Moreover, the Association of American Agricultural Colleges and Experiment Stations stressed during these early years that extension teaching should encompass *all* the problems of country life. At-

tention to rural institutions and improvement of the aesthetic side
of farm life, it emphasized, were just as important as concern with
better production and marketing.[9]

Similarly, the Department of Agriculture's program of cooperative demonstrations was originally concerned with improving
the living conditions of farmers as well as their productive
efficiency. Knapp and others also affirmed that improved farming
was but the means to a better, more comfortable country life.
Although there was a tendency to stress higher economic rewards
first and a better social life second, the Knapp program did include
demonstrations aimed at improving the efficiency and attractiveness of farm homes and cooperative work with boys' and girls'
clubs sponsored by the rural schools.[10]

When the extension service was unified under the Smith-
Lever legislation, many reformers expected the system to continue
to attach importance to the social side of country life as well as
the economic side. Indeed, home demonstration work and boys'
and girls' club work, the forerunner of today's 4-H movement,
were supported by some of the system's funds. Furthermore, the
agricultural colleges in charge of the training of demonstration
agents attempted to give them a social outlook by requiring them
to take courses in rural sociology and social oganization. But
how far agents would, and could, go in the direction of organizing
projects of a social nature was not clear.[11]

The outbreak of the First World War delayed the resolution
of this matter, for in the context of the wartime emergency, an
emphasis on improved production at the expense of social organization seemed wholly justifiable. It is true that club and home
demonstration work grew during the war years, but they also
stressed production to meet the emergency situation. Both membership and activity declined when the end of the war eliminated
the crisis as a reason for young people to join and when extra
wartime funds were withdrawn. However, this is not to imply
that the extension service gave no consideration to the social
aspect of country life. After the war, it continued to give some
demonstrations concerned with such matters as farm home re-
modeling, sanitation, and recreation, but its primary emphasis
was on improving the farmers' business.[12]

A major effect of the wartime experience upon the extension
service, therefore, was the domination of it by those people who

stressed the economic circumstances of agriculture and the use of pressure politics to produce changes. From the beginning of the educational extension activity, government agents worked with local groups, rather exclusively businessmen at first, but including some of the more prosperous and progressive farmers after 1914. Both the land grant college extension officials and the Department of Agriculture administrators encouraged the organization of these local associations as a means to facilitate the agents' contact with the communities in which they worked. Designated eventually as "farm bureaus," these groups were expected to develop an active community spirit, and, indeed, many people in the country life movement hoped they would ultimately federate all the forces working for rural betterment. But that did not happen since the extension idea which started as an educational work with concern for both the economic and social aspects of farming was changed so that its emphasis was on production and the commercial activities of farmers. Therefore, when the American Farm Bureau Federation was formed in 1920, it was a unification of only those groups concerned primarily with the farmers' economic problems.[13]

In considering the development of the extension service, it is not difficult to support a conclusion that such work was probably more successful as it *did stress* the business side of farming. For in an increasingly commercialized economy, men of the soil could understand and appreciate the demonstrated relationship between greater profits and efficient, scientific methods. On the other hand, they less easily saw the gains that might come from improved home life conditions. Moreover, there is evidence that many farmers believed that more income was all that was needed, since it would permit them to purchase telephones, household conveniences, fashionable clothing, and automobiles, which, for the most part, would solve their social problems.[14]

*   *   *

Like surveys and educational extension work, rural life conferences were recommended by reformers as a way to improve rural conditions, since such gatherings could serve as disseminators of information, stimulate people to action, and provide for a valuable exchange of ideas and experiences. Kenyon Butterfield promoted one of the earliest rural life conferences, which met at Michigan Agricultural College in 1902 to consider the social and economic problems of farmers. Subsequently, he was successful in organizing similar conferences at Rhode Island College of Agriculture in 1904 and at Massachusetts Agricultural College in 1907. Like Bailey and his work with the survey, Butterfield pioneered the conference idea some years before the Country Life Commission included it as a recommendation in its report.[15]

Beginning in 1908 there were innumerable state conferences held across the country under the auspices of a variety of reform groups. The University of Virginia began holding country life meetings in 1908, which brought together people from all over the South to discuss the special rural problems peculiar to that section. In 1910 the Minnesota Conservation and Agricultural Development Congress met in Minneapolis with such prominent Progressives and conservationists as Father John Ireland, Dr. Harvey W. Wiley, and Dr. Charles Van Hise in attendance. The following year conferences were held in Wisconsin and neighboring Illinois. The Wisconsin meeting was held jointly with "farmers' week" at the state university, while the conference in Illinois was the outgrowth of efforts by the Country Teachers' Association. West Virginia, Maryland, and Pennsylvania held conferences in 1912, the next year Michigan and Missouri convened their first state meetings, and in 1914, Iowa, South Dakota, Montana, Kentucky, and Ohio all held country life conferences.[16]

In some places, interstate or regional conferences were tried. The St. Joseph, Missouri, Commerce Club sponsored one of the first of these in 1913. People from the farms and towns of Nebraska, Iowa, Kansas, and Missouri attended "to renew the bond of sympathy between the city and the country" and to inform farmers of the best methods for making their enterprise both profitable and satisfying.[17] In 1912, the Spokane, Washington, Chamber of Commerce, along with the country life commissions of Washington, Idaho, Montana, and Oregon, sponsored another of these interstate conferences.[18] One of the most popular exhibits at this meeting was a model kitchen set up by the Grange to show how a farm housewife might save three hundred to four hundred miles of walking each year by having her work area conveniently and efficiently arranged. The New England Conference on Rural Progress, which began to hold annual meetings in 1908, was yet another regional conference. An outgrowth of Butterfield's efforts to federate the agencies and organizations working for country life improvement in the New England area, the conference changed its designation in 1913 to the New England Federation for Rural Progress.[19]

School administrators and teachers' organizations sponsored many of the early conferences, for they viewed them as a way to improve both country life and the country school. In 1909, F. A. Cotton, State Superintendent of Education in Indiana, invited the country schools of his state and four surrounding ones to convene to consider ways in which they might "further the love of country life" among rural pupils.[20] In the same year, the Superintendent of Oklahoma's schools called a meeting to consider ways to improve rural conditions and stimulate farmer interest in a better country life.[21] Sponsored by an organization called the Southwest Interstate Commission on Country Life, the conference had people in attendance from a seven-state area. Even more impressive, however, was the National Conference on Rural Education held at the University of Pennsylvania in 1917, which had representatives attending from most of the states of the Union.[22]

Churches also adopted the conference approach. While their meetings placed a major emphasis on the country church, they also concerned other aspects of the rural life situation. The proper training of country pastors elicited a great deal of discussion at these conferences, and participants generally concluded that rural ministers needed some work in agricultural subjects to prepare them for their task of revitalizing the country church. Therefore, conferences were sometimes called in order to give ministers instruction in agricultural economics, rural sociology, or farming methods. The California Agricultural College at Davis, for example, sponsored a "ministers' week," during which clergymen listened to lectures and saw practical demonstrations aimed at providing them with the background necessary to create rapport with farmers.[23]

Business organizations sometimes sponsored country life conferences to demonstrate their interest in the farmers' problems and welfare. Chambers of Commerce in towns and cities across the nation promoted meetings such as those noted earlier convened by the Spokane and St. Joseph chambers. State and national bankers' associations were also active in country life conference work. Their meetings considered numerous aspects of agriculture and rural life, but there was generally an emphasis on the role of bankers in making farming more efficient and country life more satisfying.[24]

Some conferences had the express purpose of training country life leadership. One of the first examples of this was the School for Leadership in Country Life, established in 1910 by the New York State College of Agriculture at Cornell. Reflecting the influence of Liberty Hyde Bailey's work as director of the college, it annually offered a ten-day course during the summer to ministers, librarians, and other rural leaders, which included training in rural sociology, ethics, and extension teaching. In a similar way the Massachusetts Agricultural College extended its summer conference program in 1913 to include a two-week school for the training of rural social workers.[25]

An outgrowth of these many conferences was the establishment by a number of states of country life commissions in emulation of the one appointed by Roosevelt. Unlike the original commission, however, these state commissions had funds granted for their work. In the case of the California commission established in 1911, for example, a generous $100,000 was appropriated for its work. The state commission idea seemed most popular in the West and Northwest, for besides the one in California, commissions were created in Washington, Idaho, Montana, Oregon, and Nebraska.[26]

But from the beginning, the local, state, and national conferences were held in chaotic fashion without any overall direction or coordination. Wastefulness, inefficient overlapping, and duplication were the results. To correct this, organization of all groups and agencies interested in agriculture and country life into one great movement for rural progress was advocated. Butterfield took the lead in pleading this need for federation, and his work in the Northeast resulted in the establishment of the Rhode Island League for Rural Progress in 1906 and of the New England Conference for Rural Progress in the following year. Not long after that, the Pennsylvania Rural Progress Association and the Illinois Federation for Country Life Progress also achieved some success in federating at the state level.[27]

The real goal, however, was countrywide consolidation, and the National Corn Exposition's fourth annual meeting in 1911 came nearest to the realization of the aim, since the groups present and the discussions held virtually constituted a national country life conference. But that meeting resulted in no permanent organization, and the climax to efforts to federate was not reached until January, 1919, when the first national Country Life Conference met in Baltimore. Later that year a second meeting was held in Chicago, and at that time the National Country Life Association was formally organized, with Kenyon Butterfield as president.[28]

However, the National Country Life Association was only a partial fulfillment of the goal to federate all organizations working for agricultural improvement and country life betterment. The people who attended the 1919 meetings were for the most part rural sociologists, educators, clergymen, officials from the United States Department of Agriculture and the Bureau of Education, and men and women from humanitarian and social welfare organizations. There were few businessmen, representatives of farm organizations, or proponents of agriculture as a business present at the meetings. Apparently the new federation was meant to be a consolidation of only those groups and agencies which stressed the social aspects of country living. The Country Life Association admitted the need for "reasonable economic prosperity," but it emphasized that "the end of all effort for economic effectiveness is human welfare and not merely the possibilities for more profit —not merely ease and comfort, but the values of the higher life."[29]

The development represented the working out of one of the contradictory themes of the country life movement: as the American Farm Bureau Federation was the union of those who emphasized that agriculture was a business above all else, those in the National Country Life Association represented the consolidation of groups which affirmed that farming was primarily a way of life. The divergent viewpoints were irreconcilable and, therefore, instead of permitting reformers to formulate a viable ideology for their movement, each position became the basis of a separate ideology. The events of 1919–1920 were bound to happen sooner or later.

* * *

Country life reformers believed that rural deficiencies would not be removed until public awareness prompted people to act to eliminate them. Conferences, extension education, and published results of surveys helped promote this awareness, but more was needed. As the Country Life Commission stated in its report, "some means or agency for the guidance or public opinion" was

needed.[30] From the beginning, therefore, the country life movement had its "muckrakers," whose task was to stir public awareness by revealing rural inadequacies. Reformers were confident
that once the popular conscience was aroused, its force would be
exerted until all rural shortcomings were eliminated.

Generally, this publicity of rural problems took the form of
editorials and feature articles in popular magazines. During the
period such magazines as the *Independent, World's Work, Outlook, Review of Reviews, Survey, Popular Science Monthly,* and
Collier's published innumerable special stories on agriculture and
country life problems.[31] Often these articles were the published
findings of surveys, accounts of country life conferences, and
descriptions of demonstration work. Admittedly, many of the
problems considered in this flood of writing had been causes of
complaint in the rural press for decades, but that should not
detract from the work of the country life movement in broadening
the discussion. Indeed, these articles may have brought some
urbanites their first awareness of particular rural problems.

After release of the Country Life Commission's report in
February, 1909, the publicity given to agricultural subjects increased remarkably. Some magazines devoted sections, even entire issues, to rural problems. An example was the April 10, 1909,
number of *Outlook* magazine, which filled nearly half of its pages
with country life articles written about the general theme "The
Life of the Farmer." Similarly, a part of the November, 1911,
issue of *World's Work* was a discussion of agricultural problems.
In that number the editors, desiring to promote back-to-the-land
efforts, agreed to provide information to anyone who seriously
wanted to go into farming. Response was so encouraging that a
feature dealing with problems related to farming for beginners
was added in February, 1912, and it remained a part of the
magazine's format until March, 1914. Still another rural life
number was the *Annals of the American Academy of Political
and Social Science* for March, 1912. All of its nearly three
hundred pages were devoted to country life. More than half of
the articles concerned rural social problems and revealed the
strong influence of rural sociologists on the publicist phase of
the reform movement.

What impact this publicizing of rural problems had on the
popular mind is difficult to determine with accuracy. There were

so many issues raised by reformers, and each elicited a variety of responses. Some people agreed that there were farm problems which needed attention, but others ridiculed country life publicity or were indifferent to it. Therefore, possibly the best that can be done is to suggest what seemed to be some widely held attitudes.

Certainly resentment of the exposure of farm life deficiencies as "rural slumming" was a pronounced reaction in some quarters. Contrary to what one might expect, this was not exclusively a farmer attitude. Some urbanites, for example, challenged the view that farmers were a benighted and deprived group since they were obviously the beneficiaries of so much scientific technology and high farm prices. Others pointed out that there were at least as many problems in the city as there were in the country, and they suggested that perhaps reformers ought to give more attention to them.[32] Probably the following viewpoint expressed by Melville Stone, General Manager of the Associated Press, which is in the same vein, also had its adherents among the general public:

. . . it sometimes occurs to me that perhaps the affairs of this world would get on quite as well if some of the self-appointed conservators of public morals would let the dear people exercise their own intelligence and determine for themselves what are their misfortunes and how their needs may be met.[33]

Complaints about the emphasis country life publicists allegedly gave to the social and ethical sides of rural problems rather than to economic considerations which critics thought were obviously more fundamental seemed to be a second common response. Reflecting earlier Populist attitudes, this accusation implied that reformers were not dealing with such real farm problems as the exploitation of farmers by the tariff and monopoly. However, many who made the charge probably had in mind the supposed neglect of the farmers' production and market situation. In any event, this kind of reaction was not restricted to farmers or the farm press, but characterized urban opinion as well. Nor did it follow any discernible geographical or commodity interest lines.[34]

Another prominent attitude was the antipathy toward proposals that the federal government enlarge the extent of its aid to agriculture. Typically, one editor inquired whether the government needed to get "so fatherly that its scope includes the hired girl, the hired man, and the sewing society?"[35] Such paternalism, it was argued, would destroy the farmer's independence, which was an important part of his uniqueness. Besides it would be a socialistic reversal of the theory that people should govern and take care of themselves through agencies of their own creation. Critics therefore maintained that even if some genuine country life problems did exist, and they often admitted that some did, they would be better resolved at the local level than by the national government.[36]

The tendency of country life publicists to urge that the rural exodus be retarded, even reversed, brought still another unsympathetic reaction. Critics insisted that the migration to the city was the result of economic changes generated by the industrial revolution and no amount of well-intentioned propaganda could check it. To these people, it seemed obvious that improved machinery, mass production, and the division of labor called for a reduction of the rural population by making farmers more productive per man. Moreover, the fact that farm prices were not higher than they were seemed evidence that there were still too many people engaged in agriculture. What was needed, critics maintained, was not more men on the farm but more intelligent farming.[37]

Of course, there were many people who supported country life objectives and believed the wider publicity of rural problems was long overdue. Apparently most of these were people who held conservative convictions as to the means to be used for social amelioration, since they made no insistent demand that reforms be implemented through governmental action. Therefore, sympathetic supporters tended primarily to swell the chorus urging farmers to improve conditions through their own initiative and community action, but some of them were not very optimistic about the outcome. For example, one expressed the opinion that most farmers lived in an impenetrable "atmosphere of self-satisfaction" which made it all but impossible to interest them in uplifting themselves.[38]

In view of the evidence of such divided responses to the publicity given rural problems, it appears that country life "muckraking" did not create a general opinion demanding implementation of the correctives for alleged deficiencies proposed by reformers. For the most part, the publicity only seemed to reinforce previously held opinions. Those who were already sympathetic to reform sentiment now had a growing body of literature to buttress their position, while others who were unsympathetic or indifferent remained, for the most part, unconvinced of the necessity for rural changes. As to the number who were sympathetic, it can only be guessed, but it is very probable that many Americans then, as now, knew little and cared less about agricultural problems.

* * *

Surveys, extension work, conferences, and a campaign of publicity could all rely for their promotion on voluntary effort, but some rural improvements seemed to call for governmental action. Certain others, reformers believed, would definitely be more effectively implemented with the aid of the government. Obviously such demands as those for a parcel post system, postal savings banks, a rural credit program, an engineering service to advise states on road building, and control of interstate liquor traffic[39] required federal legislation. Some, the proposed organization of cooperative associations among farmers, for example, needed both state and national laws to facilitate their development as well as to legalize their existence.

On the other hand, the national government might assist reform without using legislation. It could, for example, use the Department of Agriculture to encourage rural surveys and extension work. Congress could investigate the middleman system and absentee ownership or the control of land, streams, and forests and then enact measures if they were warranted. An agency already in existence could be given the task of educating public opinion concerning farm problems. The Bureau of Education might be enlarged and reorganized in such a way that it would become a vast collecting, distributing, and investigating establishment. And the federal government could work out arrangements with the states to allow for more effective control of public health throughout the nation.[40]

As a means of rural improvement, legislation and government-sponsored assistance were unusually successful during the early twentieth century. Many measures important to farming and rural life were passed, beginning with the Newlands Reclamation Act in 1902 and continuing uninterruptedly to the 1920s, when presidential vetoes temporarily imposed a check. In 1906, farmers and other shippers benefitted from the initiation of effective railroad regulation, and the host of patent medicine users said to reside in rural areas were afforded some protection by the passage of the Pure Food and Drug Act. Presumably, farmers would have profited from the reduced rates of the Underwood-Simmons Tariff had the First World War not occurred. Even a special consideration was given to agriculturists in 1914, when a provision of the Clayton Act exempted farm organizations from the antitrust laws. And farmers, along with the general public, received some benefit from the more stable currency and easier credit arrangements provided by the Federal Reserve System.[41]

The list of specifically agricultural legislation is even more impressive. Under the Taft administration post office facilities were expanded to include parcel post and postal savings, an incessant country life demand. Legislative landmarks for many rural reformers were set in 1913, when the Offices of Markets and Rural Organization were established in the Department of Agriculture to help farmers with marketing and organizational problems. In 1916, the Federal Aid Road Bill set uniform standards for highway construction and initiated the federal funding of road building. Likewise, the promotion of extension education and the subsidization of agricultural and domestic science education in the public schools were realized in the Smith-Lever Act of 1914 and the Smith-Hughes Act of 1917. Even more important to many reformers was the passage of the Federal Farm Loan and Warehouse acts of 1916, which helped expand agricultural credit. And although national legislation encouraging cooperative organization did not come within the period of this study, it was enacted shortly thereafter as the Capper-Volstead Act of 1922.[42]

Imposing as all these measures are, it is difficult to determine the exact influence of country life forces on the passage of either the general laws which benefitted farmers or the specifically agricultural legislation. Part of the reason for this is that other reformist groups were also working for these measures although with different aims in mind. Therefore, reformers in the broader Progressive movement probably contributed greatly to the realization of some of the goals of the country life movement. Furthermore, some of the changes supported by rural life reformers had been advocated since the late nineteenth century, and the country life movement undoubtedly benefitted from the years of agitation and the return of economic prosperity. Perhaps the best conclusion is that many of these laws probably would have been passed eventually, but the support of rural life reformers accelerated their enactment.

On the surface, the concern of country life forces with legislation as a method to ameliorate rural conditions seems inconsistent, almost schizophrenic. For while paying constant lip service to the farmers' uniqueness derived from his independence and individuality, reformers demanded government aid for him. However, this only seems to demonstrate once more the dichotomous nature of so much of country life thought: looking backward to a time that may never have existed, yet forward to a world where efficiency and social-mindedness held sway.

chapter seven

Rural Responses

What was the rural reaction to the barrage of propaganda and the numerous efforts on behalf of country residents? In particular, what did farmers think of them? How did they respond to suggestions that the rural school be changed and to the idea of demonstration work? What was their reaction to the exhortations to rejuvenate the country church and to make it concern itself with social matters more than with theological ones? Did farmers feel that bad roads were one of the roots of the rural problem and were they ready to work together in support of "good roads" efforts? What of the charges that farm life was lonely, stultifying, and devoid of inspiration—did farmers agree and were they willing to act to alleviate such conditions? Were farmers eager to accept the practices of scientific agriculture with the promises they held out? What was the rural reaction to accusations that country life was not as healthy as it might be and the importuning to be more concerned with sanitation matters? And what of the rural press and farm organizations—how did they respond to the rural life assessments and activities of reformers?

Complete or entirely satisfactory answers to these questions cannot be given, for the obvious reason that it is impossible to know what the rural populace as a whole was thinking. However, letters from farmers, editorial comment in farm journals, discussions of country life reform proposals and activities in the rural press, and statements by farm organizations and their representatives do reflect views on these matters. Letters to editors from farm people and farmer responses to the Country Life Commission's work in 1908 are especially important as indicators of opinions and desires at the grass roots.

If these letters are valid criteria, it would seem there were many farmers who actually resented the rural uplift efforts of the educators, ministers, professional rural leaders, businessmen, and others in the country life movement. A widely held attitude was that what agriculture most needed was money and with that need granted, farmers themselves would be able to look out for their own uplift. A farmer who wrote to Liberty Hyde Bailey at the time the Country Life Commission was conducting its investigation maintained that if the farmer could get justice, the social part would take care of itself. "The reason he does not provide for better sanitation, for better social privileges," he argued, was because "he does not get his due and cannot afford it."[1] Another farm resident stated the matter even more bluntly when he described the talk about uplifting the farmer as "pure rot" and insisted that all that was needed was for the farmers to get a fair deal. Obviously provoked by the statements of country life reformers, he declared that farmers did not require better conditions so much as "some means of teaching a lot of fools how infinitely more blessed and happy is the average farmer and his family than the average city laborer of the same capital and income."[2] Yet another tiller of the soil objected to farmers being told how to spend their money. "Give us a chance to make money," he wrote, "and let [sic] the spending to us."[3]

Implicit in the farmers' responses that they needed more economic justice but could take care of themselves otherwise was irritation that they had been set apart as a class needing uplift. To many farmers it seemed more appropriate for reformers to be concerned about other segments of the population, in particular, the urban indigent. Typically, one farmer related that he had read that there were thousands of people in New York City who slept in rooms without ventilation because there were no windows, and he suggested, with bitter humor, that reformers investigate and "form some plans to pump some fresh air into those dens."[4]

Many country life reformers looked upon the concern about

economic considerations as crass materialism and they would have agreed with the statement of the nature-study enthusiast, Anna Botsford Comstock, who wrote in 1905 that "the man or woman who looks after dollars and cents alone is narrow and sordid, and lives in a prison of thick walls of selfishness and looked out on the world thru a window darkened by avarice."[5] To men of the soil who tied the success of farming to maintaining a position in the economic race, such expressions probably seemed to be so much nonsense. One of Liberty Hyde Bailey's farm correspondents said as much when he wrote that some people might think the stress given the money-making side of farming was sordid materialism, but it was foolish to talk to people about the aesthetic side of life "when they are in a nip-and-tuck struggle" to keep "the wolf from the door."[6] While most farmers were probably not as desperate as this since these were years of high farm prices and general agricultural prosperity, some farmers were apparently quite poor, which reflected the fact, pointed out earlier, that agricultural conditions varied considerably.

More importantly, the foregoing responses of farmers suggest that country life reformers lacked actual roots in the workaday rural world and therefore were without any real rapport with farmers. Removed from immediate contact with the soil and not harrassed by the difficulties that beset those in farming, they appeared to be both urban and condescending to many farm people. Their advice, moreover, was unsolicited and given with self-assumed wisdom. Had the situation been reversed, probably large numbers of city men would have resented the exhortations and considered them foolish. In any event, the deep-seated suspiciousness of the rural mind, nurtured by habitual reliance upon intuitiveness, individual judgment, and the constant references to rural uniqueness, was given full rein by some farmers. The result was that many questioned the sincerity of urban reform efforts and alleged that even where intentions were good, the work was carried on in a patronizing way.[7]

Certain representatives of the rural press, no doubt reflecting opinions of readers and subtly influenced by notions of editors and publishers as to what their subscribers wanted or expected to read, reinforced the farmers' positions. Often hostile to the intrusions of urban interests into rural affairs, they questioned the motives of reformers and denounced the allegedly condescending manner of urban reform efforts aimed at improving country life.[8] Revealing indications of farm press attitudes were sometimes found in comments in urban periodicals sympathetic to country life reform activities. An example was an editorial in the *Independent* magazine, one of the country life movement's strongest press supporters, which took farm publications to task for being sarcastic and jeering about suggestions that something was wrong with farm life. The editor reacted in particular to the charge of an unidentified farm newspaper that it was ridiculous for "a lot of Eastern dreamers" to tell farmers what to do, for farmers could easily give the wealthiest man in Washington a lesson on how to be happy.[9] Certainly the frustration of reformers is understandable but they actually deserved a portion of the blame for the situation, since many of them had alienated segments of the rural press by impatiently reproaching them for being so narrowly concerned with the technical aspects of agriculture. Reformers were not very forgiving of the "tardiness" of many agricultural journals in their recognition of actual social deficiencies in rural life.[10]

Of the farm organizations which existed at the time, the Grange seemed most antagonistic toward the efforts of urban reformers. Perhaps this stemmed from resentment at what seemed to be the usurpation of its role, since the Grange from its beginning emphasized the social aspect of farm life. Worthy Overseer Nahum J. Bachelder probably spoke for most Grange members in 1908, when he maintained that the Patrons of Husbandry was a "country life commission" of its own authority and one that was more attuned to actual rural conditions than any other group.[11] Scorning urban benevolence toward farmers, he suggested that "uplift" be tried upon such people as "legislators, governors, trust magnates, stock gamblers, railroad wreckers and rich malefactors." If there were any truth to the accumulated evidence of the times, he declared, such people certainly needed it. Furthermore, he asserted, it might be well for the Grange to appoint a "Commission on City Life" and ask farmers and some others to report on conditions of urban existence. While the Worthy Overseer admitted that he did not know what exactly should be done to uplift city dwellers, he made the familiar charge that there was more need of it in the city than in the country.

Moreover, at a later date the Grange took Secretary of Agriculture David F. Houston to task for pointing out country life shortcomings. Challenging the accuracy of the secretary's statements, the editors of the *National Grange Monthly* delineated the crux of the matter when they declared that the acceptance of Houston's analysis of the situation would be an admission "that fifty years of Grange effort for rural improvement had been a flat failure." This they were unwilling to do.[12]

Apparently a great deal of the work of the state agricultural colleges and the United States Department of Agriculture also went unheeded by large numbers of the tillers of the soil. One farmer, writing in the *Outlook* magazine in 1909, estimated that not more than "one-half of one per cent" of the farmers of his state were in touch with the state agricultural college and experiment station.[13] The nature of the work of these agencies was practically unknown to the masses of farmers, he maintained, and as for the United States Department of Agriculture, it had only "nibbled at the edges of its sphere of usefulness." Although it was providing some service to farmers, he believed it had squandered millions of dollars in distributing seeds which might have been better spent on the selecting, grading, and cleaning of seeds. Another farmer stated that the instruction contained in the publications of the federal and state departments of agriculture did not always reach those who most needed to become aware that the old methods were unprofitable and even when it did, it was often not very clear. He suggested, therefore, that a series of simple leaflets be prepared and distributed wholesale across the country. These should be prepared, he recommended, "by some wise man who knows, in conjunction with some ignorant man who does not know, so that they will not shoot above our heads."[14]

Farm organizations were also dissatisfied with the state agricultural colleges and the state and federal departments of agriculture. The Wisconsin Society of Equity probably voiced the opinion of other farm organizations near the turn of the century when it described the state agricultural college as "a cold-storage institution of dead languages and useless learning which costs several millions of bushels of wheat each year."[15] A main grievance of farm organizations and some farmers was that agricultural colleges and departments of agriculture were too concerned with efficiency of production as a means of bettering the farmers' position when they should have been attempting to solve farm marketing and distribution problems. The stress on production was viewed by farm organizations as actually detrimental because it created surpluses which lowered farm prices. Agricultural colleges and departments of agriculture, as well as many farmers, were slow to recognize this situation. Farm organizations also complained that agricultural colleges, by their ill-suited programs, made farm youths lose their taste for rural life rather than fitting them for it. Interestingly, Liberty Hyde Bailey provided a partial rebuttal to this argument with a survey of agricultural college students at Cornell showing that the vast majority of them planned to return to farming or some farm-related occupation.[16]

The Country Life Commision and its work in 1908 elicited some of the strongest rural reaction to urban-sponsored reform efforts. There were admittedly varying degrees of approval of the project, but examination of comments in the rural press, and the number of unsympathetic letters in the private papers of commision members leave little doubt that there was much opposition among men of the soil. Chairman Bailey himself gave support to this conclusion when he scolded farmers for taking unwarranted offense at proposals to improve country life conditions. He stated that he would continue to believe there was need for improvement even if half the farmers of the land told him otherwise.[17]

Farmers opposed the commission for some of the same reasons that they were objecting to the country life movement in general: it was not needed since farmers could take care of themselves; the real need was for more money in the farmers' pockets; and the commission would do better to investigate and ameliorate urban slum conditions.[18] One husbandman asserted that the only thing that kept the commission from being an outright impertinence was "the high character of the President and the gentlemen of the Commission."[19]

Certainly the rural press was not unanimous in support of the work of the commission. Typical statements were that it was "slumming," that its efforts would be better expended helping the urban poor, and that farmers should not be singled out as a special case for reform work.[20] At least one farm journal deplored the investigation as a paternalistic intrusion of the federal government into agricultural matters, while another dismissed it as merely a way to win farm votes in the upcoming election.[21] Still others thought the commission was a smoke screen to draw attention away from the fact that the government had not removed certain injustices which handicapped farmers. In particular, the Roosevelt administration had done nothing effective about the inequities of the tariff or the exploitive activities of industrial and financial combinations.[22] When the commission submitted its report, some journals insisted that nothing new had been discovered, for agricultural magazines had been advocating most of the specific reforms for years. They were in firm agreement with Congressman James A. Tawney, Chairman of the Appropriations Committee, that an allocation to complete and publish the investigation would be a waste of money.[23]

* * *

Farmers have generally held a sentimental devotion to education in theory, but in practice they have often been hostile to it, due in large degree to the high economic value of children on the farm. Consequently, many opposed efforts to change the rural school, especially those aimed at lengthening the school year and extending the time spent in getting a formal education.[24] Likewise, a great number of farmers resisted consolidation efforts. Many times this was related to the countrymen's sentimental attachment to "the little red school," some of which survives today in the Midwest, where there is opposition to further incorporation into still larger school units. But often it represented grievances based on higher costs and the so-called frills of the consolidated schools.[25] In addition, men and women who were school board members were sometimes loathe to give up the power and prestige they were entitled to in those positions. Regardless of the reasons for opposition, resistance to consolidation frequently took the form of objection to free transportation, which was indispensable to the consolidated school. Some farm people argued that riding to school was an indication of the degeneracy of youth, while others contended that the government had no legal obligation nor right to become "the schoolchild's coachman." Still others, mostly women, objected to the long trips in the wagons, the waiting periods at crossroads in cold weather, the possibility of improper conversations and immoral acts, and the undesirable drivers who would corrupt children with their smoking and profanity.[26]

On the other hand, the large number of farmers who charged that the rural school was the chief ailment of country life suggests that either there were real deficiencies or the incessant lectures of reformers on the need of a reoriented school had won some farm support. Whatever the cause, many farmers complained about their schools and the education which their children received. At the time of the Country Life Commission's inquiry, for example, a memorandum based on reports from the "school-house meetings" which the commission had encouraged indicated that approximately ninety-five percent of two hundred groups reporting considered their schools inadequate.[27] Moreover, a tabulation of answers to the second question on the commission's circular, "Are the schools in your neighborhood training boys and girls satisfactorily for life on the farm?" revealed that sixty percent of 53,468 farmers and their wives responded negatively. Another two percent answered "no" with some qualifications.[28]

These statistics may not be valid indicators of genuine farm opinion, for one cannot know if those who attended schoolhouse meetings and replied to questionnaires were typical. But whether representative or not, the replies did indicate a segment of contemporary rural opinion, and on the basis of evidence gleaned from other sources, it seems probable that they reflected an attitude that was more representative than unrepresentative. With that in mind, it should be instructive to examine farmer complaints about rural education to see how they compare with those of country life reformers.

Again and again farmers expressed the view that the rural school was inadequate because it educated children away from the land and left those who remained behind poorly trained for modern farm life.[29] There was much agreement that an important factor in creating the alienation of farm youth was the rural school teacher, who allegedly knew little of country life and cared even less for it. She was accused, moreover, of constantly holding up urban ideals before her pupils and encouraging them to follow urban occupations. She told the boys, for example, that if they worked hard and learned well they might someday be clerks in a store or bookkeepers in an office, and she told girls that they might become stenographers and typists.[30]

An ironic aspect of this farm opinion regarding rural teachers is that many of the men and women who taught in the country schools were farm-bred and frequently came from the very communities in which they were teaching. The complaint that they knew nothing of country living and cared little for it therefore needs qualification. Possibly some of these teachers were, like the pupils they were accused of misleading, alienated from country life; there is at least one contemporary statement which suggested this.[31] But whether this were true or not, it hardly seems fair to charge that such people knew nothing of farming or farm life. Perhaps it would have been more accurate to have stated that such men and women did not share the same outlook concerning rural life as that held by reformers and their sympathizers among the farm population.

As might be expected, farmers who criticized rural teachers and schools for failure to inculcate country life values advocated a program which would emphasize nature study and scientific agriculture in the schools and agricultural training as part of the preparation of teachers.[32] A farm resident who returned one of the commissions circulars even suggested that consideration be given to substituting nature study lessons for fairy tales in elementary reading books since the latter had no practical value.[33] Other farmers urged the creation of special agricultural schools, financed if necessary by state and federal funds.[34] Still others maintained that attendance, particularly during the winter months, ought to be compulsory.[35] One agriculturist declared thoughtfully that it was the farmers' insistence that youths leave school at an early age to do manual labor on the farm, with its implication that one only needed to know how to read and write to be successful in farming, which was causing so many farm boys to shun agriculture as an occupation.[36]

The idea of special agricultural education for farm children was not, however, universally accepted among the farm population. In a letter to the editor of the *Outlook* magazine, one rural correspondent challenged the right of school directors to spend tax money in such a way and even attacked the host of efforts aimed at keeping young people on the farms. "I think that the demand for more people to work on the farm and produce what is needed to feed the people has blinded many people in this matter," he wrote. In looking about for some means to keep more people on the land, he continued, these same individuals "have hit upon the public school" and have concluded that this was the place to commence. While he admitted that he had no children of his own and therefore the situation being discussed did not affect him personally, he nonetheless declared his objection to any plan to force young men and women to farm or live on farms if they had no desire to do so. "As long as the city is considered more attractive," he wrote, "they will go there and stay there in spite of all the education to the contrary."[37]

Resistance to demonstration farming and attempts to get farmers to use scientific methods was another manifestation of rural hostility to ideas which farmers thought originated in the heads of city men who were unfamilar with the realities of actual farming. Ignorant of the advances of applied science and not imbued with the spirit of efficiency, farmers looked with suspicion upon reformers whose interest in scientific agriculture was actuated by their concern with conservation and scientific management of resources. As noted earlier, probably much of this agrarian suspicion of experts stemmed from accustomed dependence on intuition and personal insight. Some of it was perhaps due to ignorance and the traditional conservatism that was attached to the farm population. At any rate, Seaman Knapp, the pioneer in this effort, found it necessary to work through businessmen, merchants, and bankers, who practically forced scientific farming onto agriculturists by threatening to withhold credit unless they agreed to use progressive techniques.[38]

Not all tillers of the soil were technologically reactionary, however, nor did they have to be coerced into using advanced procedures. Some, in fact, employed the same rhetoric as Liberty Hyde Bailey and the country life reformers. Like Bailey and others, they stressed the lack of proper appreciation of the soil, which resulted in "soil mining," and they urged that a portion of the produce of the soil be returned to it so as not to rob future generations of their birthright. To these people, preservation of the land's fertility was not only part of the program to combat waste and inefficiency through scientific resource management, but it was also a moral obligation. For if the soil were holy, then it followed logically that it was sinful to abuse it.[39]

The farm journals early recognized the relationship between the employment of new methods and increased profits for farmers. It was chiefly their constant lecturing and the Smith-Lever and Smith-Hughes Acts with their provisions for county agent work and secondary agricultural education which eventually overcame the farmers' reluctance to use scientific and progressive procedures. Today, in contrast to the situation near the turn of the century, most farmers are willing and ready to adopt the latest scientific innovations although a large number obviously cannot afford the most modern ways.

Only the subject of poor roads seemed to elicit as much farmer response as that of the country school and the education farm children received there. The memorandum on the reports of schoolhouse meetings in 1908 indicated that the majority of people who attended the meetings wanted better roads, apparently because they recognized their value to commerce and social life. There was, however, common complaint about the system, or lack of it, for the administration and repair of country thoroughfares and a number of reports contained recommendations for changes. Evidently some reports went into great detail, but unfortunately the Census Bureau's agent who prepared the memorandum did not elaborate upon the nature of these. Surprisingly, there was a widespread demand among farmers for governmental assistance in highway construction and administration. Morevoever, some of the Country Life Commission's farm correspondents even suggested that money for such purposes could easily be obtained by diverting funds from such "nonessential" items as river and harbor improvement, naval appropriations, the construction of an isthmian canal, and the support of the commission itself![40]

Other farm people related the road situation to the federal government's program of free mail delivery to the farmers' homesteads, when they complained bitterly that the Post Office Department sometimes withheld that service on the basis of poor roads. Common sense, they declared, indicated that it would be better to have one man travel over bad roads to deliver the mail of many householders than to have individual farmers make the trip to town over the same roads to pick up their mail at the post office.[41] One farmer wrote in irritation that if "uplift" were desired, he would be bettering himself more by "reading the news than running after the mail."[42]

People in the country may have needed good roads in order to have rural free delivery, consolidated schools, and a less isolated community life, as reformers contended, but it was apparently the recognition of the commercial value of good roads which caused most farmers to support road improvement campaigns. As business realities were thrust upon farmers, they rather quickly saw the relationship between farm profits and high transportation costs due to bad roads. It is possible, of course, that some of them also realized that they needed improved roads if they were going to share in the new ways of life being created by industrialism.

Obvious as the need for better roads seemed, there were some landowners who opposed improvement for fear that they would have to pay huge tax bills.[43] Others expressed opposition to centralizing and consolidating road administration since it was contrary to long-standing traditions of decentralized administration and local responsibility.[44] Still others resented the urban complexion of the good roads movement, stressing that the campaign was a device of urban business interests such as bicycle and automobile manufacturers. These people readily admitted that the roads in the country were not fit for pleasure driving most of the time, but they insisted that they served the farmers' needs fairly well.[45]

The relationship of poor roads to the country church situation was cited by a large number of rural people who replied to a special questionnaire sent out by the Country Life Commission. In particular, they mentioned the irregular attendance and resulting drift away from from the church caused by bad roads. This, however, was not the major reason given by farm people for the church's dwindling numbers and vitality. It was the minister, indifferent and lacking in zeal, who was cited repeatedly by farmers as the primary factor in the degeneration of the church. Some admitted that rural pastors were poorly paid, but insisted that since so many of them divided their time between churches they probably received adequate compensation for what they did in a community. What these rural people seemed to want was a full-time minister, and contrary to the conclusions of country life reformers who advocated federation of country churches, ninety percent of the respondents believed farm communities could adequately support their separate churches.[46]

Other reasons given by farmers for decline among the country churches were: the sparse and poor population in some areas; fatigue and hard conditions of life, which kept people from the church on Sunday; insufficient and inappropriate clothing for church going; sectarian quarrels; the bigotry and worn-out dogmas which could no longer attract men; and the attitude of ministers and the churches toward activities of the young, especially Sunday baseball, Saturday night dances, and the reading of the Sunday newspaper.[47] Apparently a great deal of the opposition to federation of churches derived from the exaggeration of denominational differences and local attachments, the latter often being a cemetery near a small church where relatives were buried or even the small church itself.[48]

There was also evidence that some farmers improperly interpreted the reformers' emphasis on the social mission of the church. Instead of seeing it as a call to a new allegiance and responsibility, rural believers apparently saw it only as a release from the fear of eternal punishment and the need for salvation. However, an investigation of rural church conditions in the states of Missouri, Tennessee, Kansas, New York, and Maine published in 1916 revealed that most farmers were still fundamentalists who had not accepted the "institutionalized" church idea. In fact, where ministers were better educated, popular religion liberalized, and the church's social task emphasized, there were actually fewer church-goers and a decline in the church's activities. Conversely, where church attendance was best, ministers stood opposed to the idea of a social calling for the church and still preached a concept of religion which stressed hell and damnation.[49]

Interestingly, Walter Hines Page had recognized some years earlier—and without the use of such a study—that it was futile to attempt to promote the social message as a new appeal to country people to revitalize their churches. Farmers were too individualistic, he argued. Moreover, men who no longer feared greatly for their salvation and looked upon the old theology as obsolete, should not be expected to respond to appeals to resurrect the church. In the end, Page thought, it was probably best that the country church be allowed to die.[50] Undeniably, this was an exceptional view among leaders of country life activities. It embodied, however, a recognition of certain realities and changes taking place which sentimentalism about the country church, or a belief that urban models could be superimposed upon rural institutions, precluded for others.

The breaking down of the old appeal to men's fears of divine retribution was not the only factor the 1916 study related to the decline of the country church. The study also noted that facilities for social activity outside the church, such as dance halls and secular organizations, constituted another factor relevant to the vitality of the church. Areas with the greatest number of these competing activities tended to have the smallest church attendances. On the other hand, where the church appeared strong, these other influences did not exist, which caused the researcher to conclude that the incidence of such attractions could be used as a gauge of the church's effectiveness in a community. However, the fact that young people in some areas told the inquirer that they went to church and prayer meetings simply to have something to do qualifies this conclusion, since these youths would surely have participated at least some of the time in nonchurch activities if they had existed.[51]

Although there was much concern expressed for the roads, the school, and the church when the Country Life Commission made its investigation, there is evidence that most farm people believed the real rural problem was economic, if indeed they thought a really serious problem existed at all. It is true that in general these were prosperous years on the farm and that a majority of farmers replying to the commission's circular felt that farm prices were good. But other findings of the commission and statements gleaned from letters of farmers and their wives strongly suggest that Populist attitudes were still very much alive among the men of the soil.[52] There was, for example, great unanimity of opinion respecting the insidious influence of the middleman upon farm profits.[53] Depicted as more devious than Uriah Heep, the middleman was largely an abstraction, a composite of those who handled the farmers' produce from farmyard to consumer, but that did not make the farmers' concern about his relationship to their profits any less real.

The railroads, which had become time-hallowed objects of

farm grievance, were once again singled out as the farmers' chief oppressors. Charges of injustices, inequalities, and discrimination on the part of the common carriers, as well as other middlemen, were the most universal direct complaints presented to the Country Life Commission during its investigation.[54] Likewise, farmers and their wives voted "no" overwhelmingly to Inquiry IV on the commission's circular, "Do the farmers of your neighborhood receive from the railroads, highroads, trolley line, etc., the services they should have?"[55] Significantly, the greatest dissatisfaction was in the North Central and Western states, which had been centers of Populist activity a decade and a half earlier. It was probably more than coincidental that these were also the areas where there was much opinion that farm prices and profits were not satisfactory.[56]

To remedy the abuses involving middlemen, especially the common carriers, farmers advocated regulation of railroad rates so as to make them more equitable, laws to reimburse shippers for losses due to rough handling of produce, and even the old Populist solution of government ownership of the railroads.[57] Others suggested that farmers themselves reduce the number of middlemen in the marketing process by dealing directly with wholesale firms, or that they eliminate middlemen altogether by selling directly to consumers.[58] Still other farmers recommended that the federal government control the trusts better, eliminate speculation in agricultural staples, rescind laws which allegedly protected business but put the farmer at a disadvantage, and help farmers efficiently market their products.[59]

An implication of this last suggestion was that the government should actually encourage farmers to organize to promote their interests. For a long time some reformers had been urging that farm producers cooperate to exert some control over the prices of their products, but their arguments were never persuasive enough to overcome the farmers' individualism and independence. During the early years of the century, however, when "organize or perish" became the watchword for most enterprises, farmers came to tardy recognition of the fact that the lack of organization among them was one of the major shortcomings of agriculture. As evidence of this awareness, they replied in the negative by a ratio of over four to one to the question on the commission's circular, "Are the farmers and their wives in your neighborhood satisfactorily organized to promote their mutual buying and selling interests?" Once awakened to the need for cooperative effort, farmers across America enthusiastically developed marketing and purchasing associations to protect themselves against the harsher effects of the speculative price-and-market system.[60]

Credit, as noted earlier in this study, was another subject related to successful farming, and reformers maintained that farmers lacked adequate capital resources, which seriously handicapped them in the struggle to make farming a business. Farmers, however, disputed this judgment, for they indicated by a seven to one margin in answering the commission's circular in 1908 that banking, credit, and insurance facilities were adequate.[61] This is indeed puzzling in view of the successful campaign a short time later which culminated in the overwhelming support of legislation establishing a national rural credit system. The decisive contradiction by farmers of the reformist case for an expanded rural credit program certainly challenges commonly held assumptions. Unfortunately, there is a dearth of evidence which might explain this situation.[62]

Perhaps there was a dramatic shift in farm opinion concerning credit during the years immediately after the commission's survey of country life deficiencies. Those were years of intense commercial transition for agriculture, and the awareness of the need for more money at better terms could have made a rapid and widespread impression among farm people. It is also possible that the farm sample in 1908 was not typical of opinion among the farming population at large, although one would have difficulty demonstrating this. Actually, it is hard to imagine that there could have been much dissatisfaction among farmers with the existing credit arrangements in view of the great amount of satisfaction expressed by those who responded to the commission's questionnaire. It might be another possibility that the legislation passed during Wilson's administration was meant to benefit certain specific farm elements who exercised a power and influence disproportionate to their numbers. Or, it may be that the program for expanded rural credit represented the fulfillment of a reform aspiration for farmers without any direct relationship to widespread farmer desires. This conjecture suggests, of course, that urban-sponsored reform proposals did not always have a relationship to reality down on the farm, which is one of the conclusions of the present study.

Country people did seem to recognize an advantage to be gained by the utilization of the post offices of the land as depositories for their savings, and next to the request for parcel post, the demand for postal savings banks was the most widely called for by farmers at the schoolhouse meetings held in 1908.[63] The fact that many of the people at these meetings coupled their desire for postal savings with the wish that the funds accumulated would be made available to farmers for loans at small interest only adds to the confused position of farmers on the subject of credit. Perhaps the whole baffling matter is resolved by viewing the farmers' need for credit in terms of short-term versus long-term credit, since they may have considered the availability of mortgages for large, long-term loans adequate but saw a need for additional small, short-term credit. Farmers might therefore hope that the postal savings system would provide this without the implementation of an elaborate rural credit scheme. However, there is no evidence that the designers of the postal savings system ever contemplated its use as a loaning institution.

According to country life reformers, farmers had a labor problem that was definitely related to the efficiency and profitableness of their operations. The Census Bureau's tabulation of rural responses to Inquiry VIII, "Is the supply of farm labor in your neighborhood satisfactory?" supported this contention, for about two farmers declared the labor supply inadequate for every one that said it was sufficient.[64] However, when it came to commenting on the conditions surrounding hired labor (Inquiry IX), a matter plainly related to supply, farmers and their wives insisted by a ratio of nearly two and one-half to one that conditions for hired men were satisfactory. Apparently most farmers saw the problem as purely an economic one. The memorandum of contents of the reports from the schoolhouse meetings showed that the majority of farmers attending believed that competitive wages in industry that they had to pay to get hired hands were too high and caused the shortage of labor. Frequently, strongly stated resolutions were offered that the solution to the problem would be to keep young people on the farm to work, but unfortunately there was no elaboration as to how this should be done.[65]

An opinion poll conducted among Missouri farmers in 1911 revealed that about twenty-five percent of the husbandmen who responded thought the need for hired help was the greatest problem facing farmers in their state. After examining replies from every county in Missouri, the assistant secretary to the State Board of Agriculture, William L. Nelson, concluded that the labor problem rather than the failure to make money in farming was the crucial reason so many farmers in his state moved to town. The scarcity of help, he noted, was general and especially burdensome for farm women, who were usually greatly overworked.[66]

Hired laborers, themselves, had something to say about the situation, especially about their conditions of life and work on the farm and the relationship of those conditions to the matter of labor supply. Some who had been farm hands in the past recalled only fond memories, but others who were actually working as hired men roundly condemned inadequacies. Common complaints were that hours were too long, the work lacked a routine, farmers failed to use machines to lighten work, there was no time for recreation, the food served was improperly prepared and unpalatable, and the attitudes of employers were niggardly and self-serving.[67] With respect to the long hours of work, one hired hand wrote to Theodore Roosevelt that farmers apparently believed in an "eight-hour law," but they interpreted it to mean eight hours in the forenoon and eight hours in the afternoon![68] Another hired man charged that farmers used no "system" on the farm and he advocated compelling them by law to make certain changes. The crying need, he said, was for regular hours of work and rest, for mechanical appliances to lighten labor, for wholesome, well-prepared food, and for some amusement and play occasionally. Without these, he declared, farmers would continue to lack labor, for these deficiencies drove hired help as well as their own sons and daughters from the farm.[69]

Yet another farm worker, G. C. Buck of Shannon, Kansas, agreed that the great inadequacy of farming was the lack of order, and he suggested as a remedy that the different types of farm work be classified and have special rates of pay for each. In addition to this division of labor, he proposed that a system of schools with two-year courses of instruction be established to train men to be farm laborers. Norval Kemp, secretary to the

Country Life Commission, pointed out that this last proposal would be impractical since it would antagonize farmers if their hired hands were better educated than themselves. Undaunted, Buck replied that many hired men eventually became farmers, so it would work out for the best in the end.[70]

Actually, finding workers to help farmers with their chores was only part of the farm labor problem. The need for domestic help to lighten the work of farm women also seemed critical.[71] For example, among farm women who were polled by Secretary of Agriculture David Houston in 1913 and 1914, the lack of girls or women to help with the housework was the most frequent complaint. As a remedy, some of these women proposed that immigrants be used as domestics, while others suggested that the unemployed of the large cities be sent to the farms.[72] Both of these proposals seem surprising, but so does the fact that few of the women suggested that more mechanical appliances be used to lighten housework and alleviate the hired girl shortage.

The plight of farm women also appeared to involve more than a labor scarcity, since the women who responded to Houston's circular commented on their isolation, loneliness, and lack of social and educational opportunities, in addition to expressing their need for more hired help. Many rural people admitted that the conditions surrounding the lives and labors of most country women could be improved, but there were others who denied that the lot of farm women needed attention. A substantial number of those who were polled by Houston, for example, were apparently quite satisfied with country living, although many of them described some aspects of farm life unfavorably. Moreover, findings of the secretary's survey contradicted the reformers' contention that rural loneliness and dissatisfaction were due to isolation and bad roads, since women from populous parts of the East, where roads were good, frequently complained of loneliness, while others from the West, where people were scattered and the roads poor, often expressed contentment.[73]

Perhaps the women's other complaints and requests were even more significant. Some wanted scientifically planned homes with such creature comforts of modern urbanized civilization as electricity, running water, indoor plumbing, and mechanical appliances of various descriptions. But many were concerned about more mundane matters, such as the "scandalous fashions" for women or the alleged exploitive practices of doctors and druggists. Moreover, when making requests of the secretary's office, some asked for advice on vegetable gardening or a cheap substitute fuel for use in gasoline engines.[74] From this it would appear that many farm women did not view their lot in the same way rural life reformers did, for their complaints and desires seem almost frivolous when compared with the aspirations for them held by those in the country life movement.

The migration of country youth to the city was another factor that obviously had something to do with the farm labor problem, since the farmers' cheapest and most available source of workers was their own families. It was apparent, however, that the cultivators of the soil could not keep their boys "down on the farm" long before any of them had seen "Paree," and the explanation commonly offered was that young men left farming because economic opportunities were greater in the city.[75] Many of the farm women who took part in Secretary Houston's poll also blamed the farmers' lack of social esteem for driving young people from the land. They contended that "hayseed" and "rube" cartoons and jokes that impugned rustic intelligence and degraded the usefulness of agriculture might entertain city people, but they only humiliated farm children and caused them to want to leave the farm at the earliest moment. Therefore, they continued, even in the face of labor scarcity some parents encouraged their offspring to leave because they did not want them to have to work so hard for so small an economic reward and so little social recognition.[76]

One farmer, evidently provoked by the continual lecturing of reformers that farm boys should stay in the country, asked why they were constantly urging rural youth to remain on the farm when they were not there themselves.[77] Implicit was the knowledge that many of the professional rural leaders who did much of the exhorting had left the farm early in their lives. Editor Henry Wallace, whom the circumstances fitted and in whose agricultural journal the question had been raised, replied weakly that successful farm leaders did not have to be active dirt farmers. He declared, however, that they should be "imbued with farm spirit," but he did not make clear what, exactly, that meant. More importantly, Wallace admitted that there was not room enough for all country boys to stay in farming and therefore some should be encouraged to leave.[78]

In any event, generalizing about the rural labor situation and its ramifications at the turn of the century is difficult. On the one hand, it would seem that farmers needed more labor just when the rural exodus was taking large numbers from the land. The explanation commonly offered for this situation was that population growth with its increased food demands coincided with the ending of cheap land, which created the necessity for farmers to use intensive agricultural methods requiring more labor. On the other hand, it appears that attempts to stem the tide of rural migration by urging farmers to adopt changes that would make farming easier and more attractive actually eliminated the need for so many workers! The relationship of technological change to rural-urban migration is obvious. Quite possibly, some people also left farming simply because they were confused and discouraged by the increasingly complex demands imposed by complicated machinery, the price-and-market system, cost accounting, and so on.

It is equally frustrating to attempt to assess farm opinion concerning aspects of the labor matter. Some farmers and their wives complained about the need for help on the farm, while others deplored the lack of privacy when hired men ate at the family table and lived in the home. Similarly, some farmers who insisted that they needed more help to do their work adequately fretted about the use of liquor and profanity by hired hands because it could corrupt their children. And since the years near the turn of the century were a time of general agricultural prosperity, what is one to make of statements by farmers that they did not "voluntarily choose a slave's life" but worked harder than others because of economic necessity?[79]

This last statement to the contrary, there is evidence that many farmers had a deep respect for long hours of toil for relatively humble rewards and were actually offended by urban labor's incessant demands for shorter hours and higher pay. It is probably true that some rural resentment of the urban labor situation came from the realization that fewer hours at better wages would entice more farm boys to the city, but much of it probably derived from the agrarians' traditional view of work as a moral obligation, which the insistence upon conditions and terms of labor seemed an attempt to circumvent. Furthermore, shortening hours of work only gave extra time for idleness and dissipation, which would be the "ruination of any people."[80]

While certain aspects of the rural labor situation remain baffling, there is little doubt that many farmers acknowledged that rural life was deficient in social and cultural advantages. They replied in the negative by a ratio of nearly three to one to Inquiry XII of the Country Life Commission's circular, "Do the farmers and their wives and families in your neighborhood get together for mutual improvement, entertainment, and social intercourse as much as they should?"[81] The country's lack of a social spirit was attributed to a variety of causes: poor roads which kept people at home, especially in winter; lack of telephones, trolleys, and automobiles; the disappearance of young people, who were social catalysts, from rural communities; clannishness, which allowed for visits with relatives separated by long distances but precluded social gatherings with neighbors on the next farm; and a materialism which kept farmers so busy pursuing the dollar that they had no time for entertainment and socializing.[82]

Responses to special questions concerning the farmers' organizational, recreational, and social life collected during the commission's inquiry indicated that probably fewer than one-third of the total farm population belonged to an organization of any kind. In some states the proportion was apparently even less. About twenty percent of those responding to the poll indicated that they had few recreations or none whatever, and approximately seventy-five percent believed there were not enough social organizations in the country. Frequently the respondents deplored the dearth of "wholesome amusements," which probably meant that they thought there were too many dance halls, saloons, and the like in their area. However, some of these farm residents perhaps shared some of the attitudes of those country life reformers who implied that certain rural recreational activities were inconsequential. Lodge picnics, church socials, dances, neighborly visits, hunting, fishing, skating, and buggy riding were not strongly encouraged by some reformers because they were devoid of uplifting inspiration and cultural or educational content.[83]

Farmers apparently agreed with reformers that they needed

more recreation, but their problem was largely how to find time for it when they worked almost constantly to make a success of farming, or, in some cases, merely to keep together their bodies and souls. Moreover, it is questionable that the elaborate program of story telling, lectures, reading clubs, literary meetings, plays, and games planned by reformers would give much relief from the physical weariness so common to farming at that time. Besides, as a contemporary pointed out with a touch of humor, such a prospectus "would inevitably defeat its purpose by driving the exhausted merrymakers from the country to the cities for the sake of rest and quiet."[84]

Some rural residents recognized, however, that farm people usually did not have enough good literature, art, or music in their lives. An Iowa farmer stated that he thought it was imperative that country people develop an appreciation for good reading in order to cultivate taste, strengthen their reasoning, and overcome their prejudices. And, in a poignant letter which reflected the cultural and intellectual emptiness of her life, an Ohio farm woman expressed what was probably the genuine hunger of many farm people for the finer things of life and the advantages of a good education. There were, then, rural dwellers who resented the isolation and hollowness of their lives on the farm and some, like country life reformers, believed that farm homes were deficient in a number of ways.[85]

But when it came to charging that the country was not a healthy and sanitary place in which to live, the great majority of farmers took strong exception. More than 35,000 farmers and their wives replied in the affirmative to Inquiry XI of the commission's circular, "Are sanitary conditions of farms in your neighborhood satisfactory?"[86] Less than one-third of that number responded in the negative. The general attitude seemed to be that city slums were more unhealthy and unsanitary and that urban dwellers should pluck the beam from their own eyes before they spoke of the mote in the eyes of countrymen. Resentment of this sort provoked one farmer into listing health deficiencies in New York City, while a farm woman asked why doctors sent their patients to the country to regain their health if conditions there were so bad?[87]

Those rural residents among the minority who believed that there were health and sanitation problems in the country cited the prevalence of typhoid fever, flies, and the use of patent medicines as common health hazards on the farm. Other allegedly common farm situations were manure piles and outbuildings allowed to drain into the water supply and dead animals permitted to rot unburied. Milk was contaminated or diseased, they contended, because no health department checks were required. Farmers' diets were poor, they stated, causing ailments due to nutritional deficiencies, and medical treatment for illnesses was either unavailable or unsought.[88]

The explanation generally offered for these conditions was the ignorance of proper sanitation and health principles among farm people. In fact, Ernest Ingersoll, the Census Bureau's agent who tabulated the responses to the Country Life Commission circular, used this as a rationale for the overwhelming denial by farmers of unsanitary conditions on the farm. He stated that farm people were simply ignorant of sanitary conditions, whereas rural schoolteachers, who were overwhelming in their criticism of the rural sanitation and health situation, came closest to "a correct judgment of the conditions on the farm."[89]

No one would really deny that some unsanitary and unhealthy conditions existed in the country, but that they were as serious and widespread as urban reformers believed was disputable. Like so many other aspects of the so-called "rural problem," it was difficult to generalize accurately for the whole country since conditions undoubtedly varied greatly from region to region and even within regions.

* * *

A survey of a southern Minnesota township in 1912 at the height of country life publicity efforts gives some insight into farmer attitudes as well as to the effectiveness of reform endeavors. George P. Warber, the investigator, found that women's work had not eased much and twenty-nine percent of the farm wives still mowed the lawn, which averaged one-eighth acre in size. One-third of the women still helped with the milking and barnyard chores. Cooperative enterprises were being tried in the community, but most farmers expressed doubt that they would be able to work together successfully for very long. Not one farmer in the township had heard of the new agitation for better of the homes, but were read by only forty-seven percent of those agricultural credit. Farm journals were received in eighty percent receiving them. Many farmers admitted reading very little of the newspaper, some stating that they read only the headlines and others reporting that they seldom read the editorials. Only four-teen percent of the farmers attended farm institutes, and the majority expressed a prejudice against agricultural practices. The schools in the community continued poor and farmers seemed most concerned about the high school in the nearby town, which they felt lowered the morals of their children. Both church membership and attendance were down. As an explanation for non-attendance, many farmers stated that they did not go to church because of the unremitting work, especially the feeding of cattle. Social distance between wealthy and poor had grown and also the distinctions between the rural population and that of the town. Young people were leaving the farm at a high rate, with girls going more often than boys. Among the adults who left, it was the men who seemed more anxious to move to town.[90]

Two other surveys conducted near the end of the period covered by this study are of interest, again for the evidence of progress or lack of it made by country life efforts to convert farmers to a better standard of living. One study included four-teen hundred homes in New York State. Only two in two hundred homes had electric washing machines, while forty of every fifty homes still used kerosene lamps. Only one family in ten took regular vacations, and respondents indicated that fourteen to eighteen hours was their regular work day. Most of the people surveyed stated that they had no contact with the county extension agent, although some said that they read bulletins from agricultural colleges as well as rural newspapers and magazines. Seventy-four homes indicated that they had labor-saving devices, which ranged from running water to carpet sweepers.[91]

The second survey involved ten thousand homes in the North and West, where the average work day, based on statements by respondents, was a little more than eleven hours. Only thirteen percent of those surveyed indicated that they had an annual vacation. Sixty percent still churned their milk, while ninety-four percent still made their own bread. Forty-three percent had no washing machines, although ninety-six percent stated that they did their own family washing. About one-third of the homes had running water.[92]

* * *

None of the foregoing is meant to obscure the fact that there were always elements of the rural population and press who supported country life reformers, the Country Life Commission's work, and uplift activities in general. There is no real evidence, however, that these people were ever in the majority or that country life efforts ever had strong popular backing among farmers. On the contrary, such activities seemed to arouse resentment and animosity more often than they won favor. Some of this may have been due to the habitual suspiciousness associated with country people, and long-standing rural-urban antipathy may also account for some of it. Or, it may have been caused by the general prosperity which permitted many farmers to believe that there was nothing seriously wrong with agriculture and rural life. Perhaps in the final analysis, it was due most of all to the fact that farmers living close to the realities of farm life were never motivated to see their situation in the same way as urban reformers who idealized country life in moral and aesthetic terms.

chapter eight

Country Life Reform: Conclusions

The activities of people in the country life movement near the turn of the century failed to arouse broad popular concern for the declining status of farmers in American life. They did not even receive wide support among farmers, whom they were supposed to benefit. Therefore, it is appropriate to assess the extent to which rural reformers succeeded in bringing about suggested changes and in turning public attention to rural questions and to conclude as to why they succeeded or failed to accomplish their fundamental purposes. As has already been pointed out, legislation which was passed to remedy certain shortcomings diagnosed by reformers was one success of country life reform, although it is difficult to determine the actual influence of the movement in gaining such laws. But did the movement have any effect upon the quality of American farm life other than certain legislative enactments?

Unquestionably, rural reformers had some limited success in promoting a capitalistic spirit among farmers. Indicative of the urban impact on rural life, it involved making farming into a business and farmers into businessmen. Those farmers who became businessmen were, however, only a certain proportion of the farm population, principally the most commercialized and even then, such farmers would have to be compared with small entrepreneurs in most instances, and not with big businessmen. The bulk of the farm population was not affected, since a great many became tenants during the period and vast numbers continued to farm in the traditional unscientific manner. For these people, farming was "a way of life," but it was hardly that of the bucolic idyll!

The country life movement also had some success in getting farmers to organize to promote their economic interests. This was especially true with respect to the organization of cooperative associations among farmers. Those in the movement who formed the Farm Bureau Federation at the end of the period covered by this study also succeeded in having farmers, primarily the most business-oriented ones, organize to promote and protect their concerns through pressure politics. Organization was actually one of the new demands forced upon farmers when they became businessmen, and as such it could not be avoided. But another part of the explanation for this success lay in the fact that farmers could readily see the economic advantage of combination, whereas they could not always recognize the particular gains which were supposed to come from other reform proposals.

Certain country life remedies for rural educational problems or deficiencies were also carried out during the period under discussion. Nature study was introduced into the elementary school curriculum, the teaching of agriculture and home economics was provided by the Smith-Hughes Act of 1917, school consolidation took place, and extension teaching at federal expense was begun under the Smith-Lever Act of 1914. Moreover, these changes brought the rural school more adequate facilities and personnel and gave some useful training in agriculture. However, the entire rural school curriculum and administrative machinery was not reorganized and directed toward the unique education for country children which reformers demanded, nor was the preparation of teachers who planned to teach in the country schools changed significantly. Some normal schools, temporarily caught up in the enthusiasm for rural educational changes posited by the country life movement, required prospective rural school teachers to take courses in agriculture, but for the most part these were transient efforts of an experimental nature.

With the exception of certain legislative accomplishments to aid agriculture, the qualified success in making a part of the

farm population businesslike, and the implementation of reforms for certain educational inadequacies, the country life
movement failed to achieve its goals. Most obviously, the movement did not stop the migration of country people to the city.
This went on unabated because it was necessary. By the middle
years of the period treated by this study farmers were producing
only eighteen percent of the national income, and there were
simply too many of them in agriculture, too many sharing the
farm income.[1] Country life reformers, who wanted to stem the
tide of rural migration or even send people back to the land,
acted out of sentiment rather than good sense. Their analysis
of the rural exodus, when they made one, was faulty, for they
attributed the precipitous decline of the rural population to the
inadequacies of farm life rather than technological changes, high
land prices, and the urban lure of higher wages and shorter
hours. The drift to the city was simply an aspect of industrialism's impact on American society, which reformers either failed
to understand or resisted because they were reluctant to see
the nation become urban and industrial at the expense of farming.[2]

The country life movement also did not prevent the urbanization of rural life from taking place. In fact, the movement
actually contributed to it by urging modern farm equipment and
creature comforts on country people. No doubt rural dwellers
desired many of the refinements of urban society and acquired
them when possible, and with the growing commercial temper
of American society during the early twentieth century, few
farmers, if any, completely escaped the thrust of the industrial
city. Reformers, however, played a role in enlarging the farm
population's acceptance of the material products of the city by
stressing that they were a means to keep progressive young
people and others on the farm. Rural reformers also contributed
to the urbanization of the farm population when they urged
farmers to become businessmen, since this involved the concomitant acceptance of many of the material values of urban life.

Tenancy, considered by many to be one of the most serious
problems facing agriculture at the turn of the century, also was
not halted by country life reformers. Instead, the trend continued to divide the farming population into two parts: a smaller,
but more dominant one composed of commercial farmers, who

farmed on a larger scale, and a bigger segment made up of landless tenants, sharecroppers, and hired hands, who either produced for the market on a small scale, subsisted, or worked for someone. At the same time that tenancy was increasing, the size of the farm unit was tending to enlarge, and the reformers' proposal to reverse both of these tendencies reflected their lack of awareness of contemporary economic realities. Industrialism demanded a reassembling of the economy, including agriculture, into larger units, and with this came changes in the tenure situation in farming. In particular, the increased mechanization and capital expenditure necessary for large-scale operations made farm ownership difficult. Undoubtedly the end of cheap land, the lack of adequate rural credit, land speculation, and the prices demanded for land were factors causing some of those without land to remain landless, but these have to be viewed against the background of industrialization and its effects.

The country life reform movement also failed to regenerate and institutionalize the country church, although it did produce some individual examples of achievement in making churches more responsive to community needs. The lack of success was due in part to the inability of reformers to make the idea of a social mission of the church as appealing as the message offered by traditional religion, which emphasized salvation from eternal punishment. Farmers seemed to prefer to have the church concerned with paving the spiritual road to Glory Land rather than the real road to the nearest market. Moreover, as rural people acquired telephones, automobiles, and better roads there was less need for the church as a social center. Various urban entertainments also competed with the church for participants and especially for the rural young people. The message of interchurch cooperation, which advocated the federation of several weak churches into a single strong one, had limited appeal because doctrinal distinctions seemed too important to farm people to submerge in ecumenism. Reformers also failed to recognize that urban-industrial evolution caused the rural church, like the country school, to lose out in the competition for the most qualified personnel. Finally, some farm people were indifferent to reform proposals simply because they thought the church, any kind of church, was irrelevant to their problems.

In some instances, reformers secured suggested changes,

but failed to achieve the desired results. Good roads, for example, did not tie the rural community more closely together so much as they brought farmers into greater contact with the city. Nor did the extension of rural free delivery stop people from leaving the farm. Instead, it eliminated the socializing which farm people did when they went to the village post office for their mail. However, the use of the party-line telephone compensated in part for this loss of a social medium. The inclusion of nature study courses in the primary grades, the teaching of scientific agriculture at the secondary school level, and the consolidation of schools admittedly upgraded the rural school program and provided some practical training, but they did not seem to promote the love of country life which reformers demanded. Extension education, which was to help all men on the land and especially those who most needed it, actually worked to benefit chiefly those who were already progressive.[3] Furthermore, the demand of reformers that rural schools become social centers seemed unnecessary in many instances since they were already that.

Obviously, then, the country life movement did not resolve the so-called "rural problem." It failed to affect American rural life in a more significant fashion than it did because of the faulty premises upon which it rested. In particular, most rural reformers could not seem to understand that the forces of industrialism were simply too powerful to stem—that it was impossible for agriculture to resist the effects of industrialization. Although reformers did not actually want to return to an earlier agriculturally oriented economy, they were unrealistic in their desire and attempts to retain virtues from the rural past in the midst of industrial change. They failed to recognize that the impact of industrialization created new attitudes among rural people and caused their increasing desertion of older ways and values.

The dichotomous nature of the movement was another factor which caused country life reform to be less effective than it might have been. Part of the movement stressed the technological and business side of agriculture as most important and worked for its improvement, while the other part believed that social factors were more vital than economic and technical considerations. As pointed out in this study, the two elements worked at cross-purposes, since making farmers into businessmen necessarily destroyed values and ideals cherished by those who wanted to preserve traditional aspects of rural living. But more importantly, the attempt to harmonize the two conflicting viewpoints caused the movement to appear contradictory and confusing and it hindered the ability of reformers to carry on an effective dialogue with farmers at the grass-roots level.

In some respects, the country life movement was not radical enough. Reformers were convinced that agriculture suffered from certain handicaps and deficiencies, but they did not advocate a massive program of government legislation to overcome them. A basic conservatism seemed to prevent this. Instead, they skirted issues, such as monopoly problems, which were important to many dirt farmers by calling for "careful studies." The request for federal cooperation rather than financial aid for the highway and extension programs are other examples of a fundamental cautiousness.[4] The reliance upon surveys and publications to expose agriculture's disadvantages and arouse public opinion rather than pursuit of pressure politics can be interpreted as still another instance where a cautious, more respectable means was used in preference to more direct and radical methods. Probably the strong academic background of the movement's personnel largely accounts for this tendency to favor intellectual methods over more radical ones.

The heavy reliance on education as a curative force for rural problems was another weakness of the movement. Education has obviously not been the panacea reformers have claimed. Like everything else, it has limitations; there are some problems of society which demand other solutions. Plainly, education could not cause people to stay on the farm when economic forces were bidding them to go. To argue otherwise is foolishness. Yet country life reformers had an almost religious faith in the ability of education to transform rural life and conditions. Again, the academic predilections of many country life leaders probably account for much of this emphasis on education as the key solution to the rural problem.

Undoubtedly the country life movement lost some of its potential support and effectiveness because it enjoyed its heyday at the same time that Progressive era debate and action reached a climax in America. The more spectacular attacks upon the trusts and corruption in government overshadowed country life reforms and took some of the interest which might have existed away from the proposals of rural reformers. As this study has shown, the two movements had much in common—a similar leadership, reforms which did not derive from economic necessity, a strong moral flavor, and a practical, scientific side—but the country life movement was much narrower and less dramatic in its manifestations and accomplishments.

Finally, many country life reformers failed to be more effective because they did not appreciate just how hard life was on the farm, how unsatisfying it was to many people to be farmers in a nation which was rapidly industrializing and becoming affluent. Their sentimentalized subscription to the agrarian myth caused them to identify the farmer as an abstraction, and because they had no contact with real conditions on the farm, they had no rapport with farmers. Therefore, their proposals for country life changes were generally impractical and sometimes bizarre, as for example, the suggestion that existing highways in rural areas be made more narrow so farmers could grow crops on the land thus reclaimed.[5]

* * *

The country life movement was part of the early twentieth-century effort of American society to reform itself and as such it sought both to preserve traditional agrarian ideals in the face of industrialism and to adapt agriculture to the modern age. That the two goals were contradictory points up a basic dilemma of the movement and provides a major explanation for its inability to be more effective. But when all is said and done, it is difficult to avoid the conclusion that the most crucial weakness of the movement was the failure of so many of its supporters to recognize that the thrust of industrialization was simply too strong to overcome.

Notes

References generally are given in abbreviated form. Full citations can be found in the Bibliography.

INTRODUCTION

1. Hofstadter, *Age of Reform*, p. 216.

CHAPTER ONE

1. Quoted in Ross, *Iowa Agriculture*, p. 118. For other discussions see Hofstadter, *Age of Reform*, pp. 109–11, and Tweton, unpublished Ph.D. dissertation, Chapter I.
2. Collins, *New Agriculture*, p. 48.
3. Casson, "New American Farmer," 598.
4. U.S. Cong., *Report, Country Life Comm.*, Senate Doc. 705, p. 21. Hereinafter cited as *Report, Country Life Comm.*
5. U.S., *Statistical Abstract, 1910*, p. 121; *1930*, p. 619.
6. U.S. Dept. Agr. *Yearbook, 1917*, pp. 606–07, 614–15, 722, 743.
7. Taeuber and Taeuber, *Changing Population of the United States*, p. 118.
8. Computations based on figures given in U.S., *Statistical Abstract, 1920*, pp. 52–54.
9. U.S. Dept. Agr., *Yearbook, 1917*, pp. 614–15.
10. U.S. Bur. Census, *Thirteenth Census, 1910*, Vol. V, *Agriculture*, pp. 28, 29; Saloutos and Hicks, *Agricultural Discontent*, pp. 22–23; Shideler, *Farm Crisis*, pp. 4–5.

11. U.S. Dept. Agr., *Yearbook, 1910,* p. 10; *Yearbook, 1917,* pp. 614–15, 606–07, 626, 743, 722.

12. Hofstadter, *Age of Reform,* p. 118.

13. *Ibid.,* p. 114.

14. *Report, Country Life Comm.,* p. 21.

15. U.S. Bur. Census, *Thirteenth Census, 1910,* Abstract, p. 55; Kuznets, *National Income,* p. 41.

16. Literature concerning the rural exodus is voluminous. The following are particularly useful in providing an understanding of the development: Gillette, "City Trend of Population"; Kinley, "Movement of Population"; "Exodus of Farmers"; Strong, *Challenge of City,* pp. 22–23; Hoagland, "Movement of Rural Population in Illinois," 913–17; Weeks, "Question of Agricultural Population."

17. Faulkner, *Decline of Laissez-Faire,* pp. 316–17; Main, "Western Land Problems," 252; L. Bailey, *State and the Farmer,* pp. 16–17.

18. Curtis, "What Is the Matter With Farming?"; "Farmers and Others"; U.S., *Statutes at Large,* XXIX, pt. 2 "Income Tax," pp. 756–57, 761–62 (December, 1915–March, 1917).

19. "Taffy for the Farmer"; U.S., *Statistical Abstract, 1920,* p. 141; Callicotte, "Discussion," pp. 971–72.

CHAPTER TWO

1. Fiske, *Challenge of the Country,* pp. 56–58, gives a list of forty institutions and agencies involved in the struggle for a better rural life. For another discussion of some of the material in this section, see Clutts, unpublished Ph.D. dissertation, pp. 6–7 and Chapter VII.

2. Saloutos and Hicks, *Agricultural Discontent,* pp. 66–67.

3. U.S. Dept. Agr., *Social and Labor Needs of Farm Women,* Rep. No. 103; *Domestic Needs of Farm Women,* Rep. No. 104; *Educational Needs of Farm Women,* Rep. No. 105; *Economic Needs of Farm Women,* Rep. No. 106; Carver, "Work of Rural Organization," 843–44; Malin, "Background of First Bills to Establish a Bureau of Markets." The Office of Rural Organization, established in 1913 and headed by T. N. Carver, was the primary agency of the Rural Organization Service. For evidence that the idea for a "rural organization service" came from Walter Hines Page, see memo to Houston from Page, March 25, 1913, Secretary of Agriculture, General Correspondence, National Archives, Records Group 16. The location of the secretary's correspondence will be cited hereafter as NA, RG 16.

4. Hall, "Country Towns"; Wright, "Hill Town Problem."

5. McConnell, *Decline of Agrarian Democracy,* pp. 24–33, contains a good summary of business efforts to promote better agricultural practices during the early years of the century. For Knapp's work, see J. Bailey, *Knapp,* and Cline, *Knapp.*

6. Lyle, "Corn Gospel Train"; Gregory, "Farming by Special Train."

7. W. W. Finley, president, Southern Railway Company, an open letter to newspaper editors in communities along the route of the

Southern Railway, September 30, 1908, in Box 1742, Pinchot MSS; "Railroad Missionary"; O. Wilson, "Railroading Knowledge to the Farmers," 106.

8. "Agriculture the True Source of Our Wealth"; "James J. Hill's Advice"; Hill, *Highways of Progress*. Hill's book appeared originally as a series of articles entitled, "Highways of Progress; What We Must Do to be Fed," in *World's Work*, XIX–XX (November, 1909–May, 1910).

9. "Interest of Bankers in Agricultural Education"; Marshall, "Bankers Find Profit in Making Better Farmers"; president's address, Illinois Bankers' Association, *Proceedings of Twenty-Second Annual Convention, 1912*. B. F. Harris, Champaign, Illinois, banker and friend of Theodore Roosevelt, was representative of those in banking who supported efforts to get a national extension system and agricultural education introduced into the school curriculum. See his article, "What I Am Trying to Do" and his correspondence in the James MSS: letter to Edmund James, president, University of Illinois, February 26, 1912, Box 27, and letter to Clayton Mark, president, Chicago Commercial Club, September 28, 1912, Box 32.

10. Marshall, "Bankers Find Profit in Making Better Farmers"; "Doctor of Agriculture—A New Profession"; B. F. Harris to Theodore Roosevelt, December 13, 1911, Series 1, Box 183, Roosevelt MSS; "Bankers and Farmers."

11. Werner, *Rosenwald*, p. 63; Emmet and Jeuck, *Catalogues and Counters*, p. 193.

12. Page, "Hookworm and Civilization"; Sullivan, *Our Times*, III, 290–332; Hendrick, *Page*, pp. 370–72.

13. *General Education Board*, pp. 17, 18–70, 179–89; Buttrick, "General Education Board"; "Plans for Rural Utopia."

14. Agresti, *Lubin;* Welliver, "Eliminating the Middleman," 65–66.

15. "Country Improvements"; L. Bailey, "Rural Development"; "Indiana 'Putting It Up' to the Public."

16. Wooley, "Woman's Club Woman," 562; "Bringing City and Farm Women Together"; Pearson, "City Rest Rooms," 27.

17. Carney, *Country Life and the Country School*, pp. 273–75, 316–18; Butterfield, *Chapters in Rural Progress*, pp. 104–20, 233–35; Pennsylvania Rural Progress Association, *Report of the President and Secretary*, December 20, 1912, in Box 1738, Pinchot MSS.

18. Carney, *Country Life and the Country School*, pp. 53–57. For progress of the Presbyterian Board of Home Missions Survey of Maryland, see letters from Herman N. Morse of the board to Willet Hays, Assistant Secretary of Agriculture, June, 1912, to January, 1913, in the secretary's correspondence, NA, RG 16. A list sent to Hays by George F. Wells, chairman of the Methodist Country Church Commission, November 22, 1913, indicated that the following denominations had rural church commissions by 1913: Congregational, Methodist, Methodist Episcopal, Moravian, Presbyterian, Protestant Episcopal, Unitarian, and United Presbyterian.

19. "Church and Rural Progress"; "Country Church." Wells,

"Rural Church," 134–136, contains a list of organizations formed to improve the country church.

20. Carney, *Country Life and the Country School,* pp. 57–60; Wells, "The Country Church," 302; Roberts and Israel, "Rural Work of the YMCA."

21. U.S. Dept. Agr., *History of Agricultural Education;* pp. 358–59, 334–35; National Education Association, *Proceedings and Addresses, 1907,* pp. 44–45; "Report of the Committee of Twelve on Rural Schools," *ibid., 1897,* pp. 385–583.

22. U.S. Dept. Agr., *History of Agricultural Education,* Parts III, IV; Monahan, "Rural Education," p. 157; order creating a "Division of Rural Education," November 1, 1911, Bureau of Education, Department of the Interior, National Archives, Records Group 122; Philander P. Claxton, Commissioner of Education, to Theodore Townsend, State Board of Education, Delaware, November 8, 1911, Bureau of Education, Department of the Interior, NA, RG 122.

23. For discussions of the rural side of the progressive education movement, see Chapter V; Keppel, unpublished Ph.D. dissertation, *passim;* Clutts, unpublished Ph.D. dissertation, pp. 207, 216–29; Cremin, *Transformation of the School,* pp. 41–50, 75–89.

24. Welliver, "Eliminating the Middleman," 67–70. See Saloutos and Hicks, *Agricultural Discontent,* Chapters V and VIII, for good brief accounts of the history of the Society of Equity and Farmers' Union, respectively. See also Barrett, for an early account by the second president of that organization, and Everitt, "New Farmers' Movement," for a statement by a founder of the Society of Equity.

25. Ellsworth, "Theodore Roosevelt's Country Life Commission," is the best published study of the commission to date. However, for other useful information see the following: Rodgers, Chapter VIII; Digby, *Plunkett,* Chapter VI; Tweton, unpublished Ph.D. dissertation, Chapters VI–VIII; and Clutts, unpublished Ph.D. dissertation, Chapters III–V.

26. *Report, Country Life Comm.,* p. 24; Ellsworth, "Theodore Roosevelt's Country Life Commission," 157–62; McGeary, *Pinchot,* p. 101; Pinchot, *Breaking New Ground,* pp. 340–41; Wallace autobiography, III, 100–01. Sir Horace Plunkett, Anglo-Irish baron, conservationist, and pioneer in the development of agricultural cooperatives in Ireland, is credited with originating the commission idea and, with Pinchot, stimulating Roosevelt's interest in it. See Pinchot to Plunkett, May 29, 1908, Pinchot MSS; "Appreciations of Sir Horace Plunkett"; Digby, *Plunkett,* p. 116; Tweton, unpublished Ph.D. dissertation, pp. 57–58, 118.

27. Roosevelt to Bailey, August 10, 1908, Roosevelt to Henry Wallace and other members of the Country Life Commission, November 9, 1908, in Morison and Blum, *Letters of Theodore Roosevelt,* VI, 1169, 1339; *Report, Country Life Comm.* pp. 25–28. Based on the minutes of Country Life Commission hearings, November 9–December 22, 1908, Box 1737, Pinchot MSS, only 38 of 320 identifiable speakers were farmers. College personnel (92) and government officials (52) were the two largest groups identified at the hearings.

28. Ellsworth, "Theodore Roosevelt's Country Life Commission," 164; "Presidential Anxiety for the Farmer," 235.

29. See, for example, *Twice-a-Week Spokesman–Review* (Spokane, Washington), August 12, 1908, December 4, 5, 6, 7, 1908; "Commission on Country Life"; "Farm Life Commission"; "Country Life Commission," *Springfield Republican;* J. H. Schneider, RFD, White Bear Lake, Minnesota, to Theodore Roosevelt, Box 1743, Pinchot MSS. "Farm Papers on Rural Uplift" contains a list of farm journals across the nation which supported the commission's work.

30. *New York Journal of Commerce, New York Evening Post,* both quoted in "Presidential Anxiety for the Farmer," 235; "Paternalism"; Peer, "What is the Matter with Agriculture?"; "Hardware Section"; "What Do the Farmers Want?"; Editorial comment, *Sacramento Union, San Francisco Chronicle; Maine Farmer* (Augusta), *Farm and Fireside* (Springfield, Ohio), *The Homestead* (Des Moines), *Farm, Stock, and Home* (Minneapolis), *National Stockman and Farmer* (Pittsburgh), *Farm and Field* (Denver), all quoted in "Farm Papers on Rural Uplift."

31. *Report, Country Life Comm.,* pp. 19, 52–55. All of these recommendations had some results: the Smith-Lever Act, which established a national extension program, accomplished the first; the new disciplines of rural economics and rural sociology owed much to the second; and the great number of country life conferences held after 1908 was an outgrowth of the third.

32. Bailey to Pinchot, January 16, 1909, Box 1741, Pinchot MSS; Ellsworth, "Theodore Roosevelt's Country Life Commission," 169–70; U.S. Congress, *Congressional Record,* 60th Cong., 2d sess., 1909, XLIII, Part 3, 3118–20, 3310; Part 4, 3660–64.

CHAPTER THREE

1. See Appendix for the list of reformers with a brief annotation for each.

2. These and the following statistics are based on data taken for the most part from Leonard and Marquis, *Who's Who in America,* and *The National Cyclopedia of American Biography, passim.* The biographical material for some of the people actually indicated that they were born or reared on the farm; in other cases, statements that birth was in a county or near a town or village implied farm origins.

3. There were 42 Bachelor of Arts, 18 Bachelor of Science, 2 Bachelor of Agricultural Science, 2 Bachelor of Divinity, 2 Bachelor of Pedagogy, 3 Bachelor of Laws, 1 Bachelor of Agriculture, 29 Master of Arts degrees, 7 Master of Science, 2 Master of Agriculture, and 2 Master of Philosophy degrees.

4. Cremin, *Transformation of the School,* pp. 119–20, 172–73, 176; Monroe, *Cyclopedia of Education,* V, 358.

5. Educators (college and public school teachers) also made up nearly one-third of the identifiable participants at the Country Life Commission hearings in 1908. See minutes for the meetings in the Pinchot MSS, Box 1737.

6. Six persons in the sample had law degrees or had passed a bar examination, but only half of these continued to practice law in the early twentieth century and only two referred to themselves as lawyers in the biographical data.

7. For example, see Davenport, *Education for Efficiency;* Earp, *Social Engineer;* Carney, *Country Life and the Country School;* Cubberly, *Improvement of Rural Schools;* Spillman, "Efficiency Movement in Its Relation to Agriculture."

8. See Mowry, *California Progressives,* Chapter IV; Mowry, *Era of Theodore Roosevelt,* Chapter V.

9. The birth date for one person could not be found; therefore, age computations are based on a sample of 83.

10. The breakdown of the sixty-three for whom religious affiliation was found is as follows: 15 Congregationalists, 11 Presbyterians, 11 Methodists, 9 Baptists, 5 Episcopalians, 3 Church of Disciples, 3 Jews, 2 Catholics, 1 Dutch Reformed, 1 Lutheran, 1 Universalist, and 1 Christian Scientist. For the statement, see J. Horace McFarland to James E. West, June 23, 1911, Series 1, Box 170 Roosevelt MSS. The emphasis was McFarland's.

11. Although exceptions, several people in the sample were quite active politically. The involvement of Theodore Roosevelt is, of course, well known. Myron Herrick, active in the effort to improve rural credit conditions, was Governor of Ohio during the early years of the century. a delegate to the Republican National Convention on several occasions, and a member of the Cleveland, Ohio, city council in the 1890s; he was also one of Marcus Hanna's lieutenants in Ohio during the latter period. Herbert Quick had warred on boodlers in Sioux City, Iowa, during the 1890s and was elected mayor at the turn of the century. John M. Gillette was a member of the Grand Forks, North Dakota, city council during World War I. Herbert Collingwood, editor of the *Rural New Yorker,* ran for governor of his state on one occasion. William L. Nelson, who was assistant secretary of agriculture for Missouri when the *Country Life Commission Report* was released, was elected a congressman from that state a short time later. An example of antipathy toward political adherence was Liberty Hyde Bailey's objection to stating his party affiliation under the direct primary law because he wanted to be "a cooperator" and not a partisan.

12. An article by Wayne Fuller, "The Rural Roots of the Progressive Leaders," places much emphasis on the rural origins of early twentieth-century reformers. Fuller maintains that their rustic antecedents fostered such attitudes as hatred of class distinctions, aversion to special privilege, and a moralistic outlook, and he concludes that "in thought and feeling the majority of them belonged to rural America." Undoubtedly the farm and village background of many reformers did influence some of their attitudes, for that is an implication of the present study. However, Fuller's analysis seems oversimplified and his stress on the rural roots of reformers overstated. He fails, for example, to give attention to those reformers who were primarily interested in building a modern civilization based on scientific management and planning. Such people did not feel, as he indicates reformers with rural origins did, that their values were threatened by a corrupt urban world. Nor does Fuller give adequate recognition to the urban impact on reform

leaders, for despite their rural upbringing they had lived or worked in cities for years and many of their attitudes had become urbanized. In the case of many country life reformers, their loss of contact with contemporary farm life was reflected in their romantic and sentimental view of rural existence, which resulted in an irrelevant assessment of much of the agricultural situation.

13. For statements of agrarian sentimentalism by country life leaders, see L. Bailey, *Country Life Movement*, p. 16; Wallace, "The Socialization of Farm Life"; Page, "The Man Who Owns the Land"; Pinchot, *Fight For Conservation*, pp. 21–22; Scudder, "Rural Recreation," 176–77.

14. Plunkett, *Rural Life Problem of the United States*, p. 44; Baruch, "Some Aspects of the Farmers' Problems," 112.

15. The following sources are useful for an understanding of the agrarian myth and agricultural fundamentalism in American history: Hofstadter, *Age of Reform*, Chapter I; Smith, *Virgin Land*, Chapters XI–XXII; Griswold, *Farming and Democracy, passim;* Johnstone, "Old Ideals Versus New Ideas."

16. Bailey, *Country Life Movement*, p. 20.

17. Wallace, "Socialization of Farm Life"; Plunkett, "Neglected Farmer," 299.

18. The realistic treatment of farm life in literature by Hamlin Garland (e.g., *Main-Travelled Roads*) and other writers just prior to the period under discussion suggests the possibility of this sort of motivation. See also, Hutchinson, "Overworked Children," 118.

19. For statements which support these conclusions, see Bisland. "Societies for Minding One's Own Business"; Mrs. Mary A. Jacobson, president, New Jersey Conference of Charities and Corrections, to Bailey, December 11, 1908, Bailey MSS; Butterfield, "Training of Rural Leaders."

20. Cubberly, *Changing Conceptions of Education*, pp. 15–16.

21. *Ibid.*

22. "Birth–Control and Race–Suicide," 244.

23. *Ibid.*, 244–45; William S. Rossiter to Theodore Roosevelt, June 12, 1911, Series 1, Box 169, Roosevelt MSS; Rossiter, "Pressure of Population," 840–43.

24. Carver, "Economic Significance of Changes in Country Population"; Carver, "Life in the Corn Belt," 4238.

25. Minutes of the Country Life Commission hearings; J. H. Hale, South Glastonbury, Connecticut, to Norval Kemp, secretary to the Country Life Commission, October 14, 1908; J. C. Simpson, secretary, Iowa Department of Agriculture, to Kemp, October 4, 1908; Barrett to Bailey, January 16, 1909, all in the Bailey MSS; Mowry, *Era of Theodore Roosevelt*, p. 93. Prior to becoming secretary to the commission, Kemp was executive director of the Society for Italian Immigrants in New York City, and during the commission's investigation he conducted an inquiry into immigration in relation to country life. Some of the responses to his inquiries are in the Bailey MSS.

26. For some expressions of these viewpoints, see L. Bailey, "Collapse of Freak Farming," 15; Hill, *Highways of Progress*, Chapter

III; Davenport, "Scientific Farming"; Henry Wallace, "Back to the Land," address given before Third National Conservation Congress, September 26, 1911, in Wallace MSS; "Farms Neglected, Houston's Warning"; Houston, *Eight Years With Wilson's Cabinet,* I, 199–200; C. Vrooman, "Agricultural Revolution," 111–12.

27. See, for example, Plunkett, "Conservation and Rural Life," 263; Plunkett, *Rural Life Problem of the United States,* pp. 150–51.

28. O. Wilson, "Railroading Knowledge to the Farmers"; Harger, "Country Banker's Awakening"; McConnell, *Decline of Agrarian Democracy,* pp. 30–32; Address of Chairman, Agricultural Committee, Iowa Bankers' Association, *Proceedings, 1912,* pp. 47–48.

29. "Commission on Country Life"; L. Bailey, *State and the Farmer,* pp. 111–32, 95, 104–05; Butterfield, *Chapters in Rural Progress,* pp. 22–27; *Report, Country Life Comm.,* p. 14; Plunkett, *Rural Life Problem of the United States,* pp. 87–91.

30. Croly, *Promise of American Life,* pp. 168–70; 267ff.; Theodore Roosevelt, Speech at Osawatomie, Kansas, August 31, 1910, in Hagedorn, *Works of Theodore Roosevelt,* XVII, 19; C, Vrooman, "Cooperation a Great Hope"; L. Bailey, *State and the Farmer,* p. 62; "For a More Satisfactory Country Life"; Sears, "Problem for the Rural School," 176.

31. *Report, Country Life Comm.,* p. 53; Carney, *Country Life and the Country School,* pp. 323–24. For other examples of the unbounded faith in the efficiency of education, see L. Bailey, "Common Schools and the Farm Youth"; Foght, "Country School," 156–57.

32. Mowry, *Era of Theodore Roosevelt,* Chapter V; Hofstadter, *Age of Reform,* Chapter IV.

33. E. D. Ross, "Roosevelt and Agriculture," 288.

34. For a general discussion of Roosevelt's attitudes toward farming and farmers, see E. D. Ross, "Roosevelt and Agriculture." For examples of Roosevelt's statements on farmers and farming, see Roosevelt to Anna Roosevelt Cowles, July 8, 1888, in Anna Roosevelt Cowles, *Letters,* p. 97; Roosevelt to John Hay, August 9, 1903, to George Otto Trevelyan, March 9, 1905, to L. H. Bailey, August 10, 1908, to Herbert Myrick, September 10, 1908, in Morison and Blum, *Letters,* III, 548, IV, 1132, VI, 1167–70, 1224–28; Roosevelt, "Rural Life"; Roosevelt, "Welfare of the Farmers."

35. Harbaugh, *Roosevelt,* pp. 18, 25; Cutright, *Roosevelt.*

36. Roosevelt, "The Man Who Works With His Hands," Address at Semicentennial of the Founding of Agricultural Colleges in the United States, Lansing, Michigan, May 31, 1908, in Hagedorn, *Works of Theodore Roosevelt,* XVI, 133.

37. For examples of Roosevelt's views on the fundamental role of agriculture and his romantic depiction of the farmer, see E. D. Ross, "Roosevelt and Agriculture," 297–98; Roosevelt to Kermit Roosevelt, June 1, 1907, to L. H. Bailey, August 10, 1908, to Herbert Myrick, September 10, 1908, in Morison and Blum, *Letters,* V, 676–77, VI, 1167–68, 1225–27; Roosevelt, *Foes of Our Own Household,* p. 113; Special Message Transmitting the Report of the Country Life Commission, February 9, 1909, *Report, Country Life Comm.* p. 9.

38. On this "race suicide" theme, see Roosevelt to Cecil Arthur Spring Rice, August 5, 1896, May 29, 1897, August 11, 1899, March 16, 1901, to Anna Roosevelt Cowles, December 17, 1899, to Albert Shaw, April 3, 1907, to William H. Taft, December 21, 1908, in Morison and Blum, *Letters,* I, 554, 620–21, II, 1053, 1112–13, III, 14–16, V, 636–38, VI, 1433–34; Roosevelt to William S. Rossiter, July 28, 1911, Series 3A, Letterbook, Volume 24, Roosevelt MSS; Hagedorn, *Works,* II, 251, XIII, 513, 636, XIX, 149.

39. Roosevelt to H. Rider Haggard, June 28, 1912, Morison and Blum, *Letters,* VII, 568; Hays, *Conservation and the Gospel of Efficiency,* pp. 2, 266–67.

40. Roosevelt, *Foes of Our Household,* p. 114.

41. See speech, Bangor, Maine, August 23, 1902, *Works of Theodore Roosevelt,* Executive Edition, XIII, 127–28; speech, Sioux Falls, South Dakota, April 6, 1903, *ibid.,* 303–05; Annual Messages, 1902, 1904, 1906 in Hagedorn, *Works,* XV, 165, 231–34, 374–76. For Roosevelt's advocacy of subsidized agricultural training, see Roosevelt to Herbert Myrick, September 10, 1908, Morison and Blum, *Letters,* VI, 1228.

42. Annual Message, 1901, in Hagedorn, *Works,* XV, 105–06; Roosevelt to Joseph G. Cannon, June 13, 1902, in Morison and Blum, *Letters,* III, 272–73; Peffer, *Closing of the Public Domain,* pp. 32–33; Robbins, *Our Landed Heritage,* pp. 330–33.

43. Annual Messages, 1901, 1902, in Hagedorn, *Works,* XV, 105–06, 161–62; U.S. Dept. Agr., *Report, Public Lands Comm.;* Roosevelt to James Wilson, Secretary of Agriculture, February 3, 1903, Morison and Blum, *Letters,* III, 416; William Kent to Roosevelt, January 29, 1909, Series 1, Box 140, Roosevelt MSS.

44. Roosevelt to John Hay, August 9, 1903, Morison and Blum, *Letters,* III, 548.

45. Roosevelt to George Otto Trevelyan, March 9, 1905, Morison and Blum, *Letters,* IV, 1132. Roosevelt wrote a similar letter to Trevelyan on June 19, 1908. See Morison and Blum, *Letters,* VI, 1087–88.

46. Ellsworth, "Theodore Roosevelt's Country Life Commission," 156; E. D. Ross, "Roosevelt and Agriculture," 301–03; speech, Bangor, Maine, August 27, 1902, *Works,* Executive Edition, XIII, 128–29; Roosevelt, "The Man Who Works With His Hands," 138–39, 141.

47. Roosevelt to Herbert Myrick, September 10, 1910, Morison and Blum, *Letters,* VI, 1225–27.

48. Hays, *Conservation and the Gospel of Efficiency,* pp. 268–69; E. D. Ross, "Roosevelt and Agriculture," 310.

CHAPTER FOUR

1. See, for example, "What Really Troubles Cornell"; Mann, "Life of Liberty Hyde Bailey," 72; H. Knapp, "Director Bailey"; McConnell, *Decline of Agrarian Democracy,* p. 191, note 3; Hays, *Response to Industrialism,* p. 111.

2. Rodgers' work on Bailey, cited earlier, and Dorf, *Bailey,* are the chief biographies. In addition, the following also provide useful

information: Mann, "Life of Liberty Hyde Bailey"; Larson, "Liberty Hyde Bailey's Impact"; Lawrence, "Bailey"; "Liberty Hyde Bailey, Botanist, Dead"; Aronovici, "Bailey."

3. Ellsworth, "Theodore Roosevelt's Country Life Commission," 158.

4. Dorf, *Bailey*, p. 110; Aronovici, "Bailey," 125–26. During the 1890s Bailey created one of the first rural extension programs in the nation, and later when a federally-sponsored extension system was realized in the Smith–Lever Act, one of the authors of the law reportedly consulted Bailey to learn his views. See U.S. Dept. Agr., *History of Agricultural Extension*, pp. 44–45; Rodgers, *Bailey*, p. 365. (Rodgers does not indicate which of the two authors of the extension act conferred with Bailey.)

5. Dorf, *Bailey*, pp. 109–15; Aronovici, "Bailey," 126.

6. Rodgers, *Bailey*, pp. 300, 351, 367; Taylor and Taylor, *Story of Agricultural Economics in the United States*, pp. 43, 54, 358–59; Brunner, *Growth of a Science*, pp. 2–3.

7. Bailey was a prodigious compiler, and his *Cyclopedia of American Agriculture* (4 volumes), *Cyclopedia of American Horticulture* (4 volumes), and *Standard Cyclopedia of American Horticulture* (6 volumes) have earned him prominence in agriculture, botany, and horticulture. He has been compared to such eighteenth-century encyclopedists as Ephraim Chambers in England and Denis Diderot in France. See Aronovici, "Bailey," 125–26.

8. Bailey, *Nature-Study Idea*, p. 96; Bailey, *Holy Earth*, p. 11; Bailey, *Outlook to Nature*, pp. 86–89.

9. *Outlook to Nature*, pp. 86–88; *State and the Farmer*, p. 172; Dorf, *Bailey*, pp. 85, 90–94; Rodgers, *Bailey*, pp. 352–53.

10. *Outlook to Nature*, pp. 6–8; *Holy Earth*, pp. 49–50.

11. *Outlook to Nature*, pp. 36–37; Dorf, *Bailey*, pp. 95, 84, 18. Bailey's father taught him to accept weather as it came since to complain about it was blasphemy.

12. Dorf, *Bailey*, p. 85; Rodgers, *Bailey*, p. 198.

13. Bailey, "Some Aspects of the Country Life Movement," 104–05; Dorf, *Bailey*, pp. 178–79; *Outlook to Nature*, pp. 1–5, 112–13.

14. *Outlook to Nature*, pp. 5–6, 92–93; Bailey, *Harvest of the Year*, p. 32.

15. *Nature-Study Idea*, p. 52; *Outlook to Nature*, p. 27; Bailey, *What is Democracy?*, p. 96; *Holy Earth*, pp. 39, 36; Bailey, *Universal Service*, pp. vii–xii, 25–27, 69; Bailey, *Seven Stars*, p. 8.

16. *Holy Earth*, passim; *Seven Stars*, pp. 100, 106; *Universal Service*, pp. 35–37, 163–65. *Holy Earth* was Bailey's testament to his profound conviction of man's obligations to the soil.

17. *What is Democracy?*, pp. 148–50; *Holy Earth*, pp. 32–34, 51–53.

18. *Outlook to Nature*, pp. 59, 33, 166, 152–53, 156; *Holy Earth*, pp. 8, 104–05, 115, 120–23, 63, 33; *State and the Farmer*, p. 69; *Country Life Movement*, pp. 19–20; *Universal Service*, pp. 164–65.

19. *Seven Stars*, pp. 18–30; *Holy Earth*, p. 63; *Outlook to Nature*, pp. 111–12. Bailey wrote more than 50 books, edited many more, and

authored innumerable articles, bulletins, and pamphlets.

20. *Country Life Movement,* p. 16; *Harvest,* pp. 48–49.

21. Mowry, *Era of Theodore Roosevelt,* Chapter V; *Universal Service,* p. 161; *Seven Stars,* pp. 3, 6, 144; *Harvest,* pp. 39–40, 82–83; *Country Life Movement,* pp. 63–74.

22. *Harvest,* pp. 29–40, 55; *Seven Stars,* pp. 60, 56.

23. *Seven Stars,* pp. 29–30; Dorf, *Bailey,* p. 231.

24. *Country Life Movement,* p. 17.

25. *Universal Service,* pp. 65, 137–38, 132–33; "Some Aspects of the Country–Life Movement," 104.

26. Dorf, *Bailey,* pp. 9, 174–75; Bailey to Roosevelt, February 9, 1916, Series 1. Box 296, Roosevelt MSS; *Universal Service,* pp. i–xii, 111, 56.

27. *Country Life Movement,* pp. 57–58.

28. In contrast to Roosevelt's flat insistence that cooperative activity among farmers did not affect their individualism, Bailey did offer the rationalization that the "individuality of one's opinions" could prevail in a group. That, to Bailey, was a newer and better type of individualism than the older kind which emphasized isolating oneself from cooperation with others. He was candid enough to admit, however, that the question of how to have cooperative action without destroying individualism was one of the most perplexing problems facing contemporary society. See *Universal Service,* pp. 162–63; *Seven Stars,* pp. 63–64; *Holy Earth,* pp. 137–38.

29. *What Is Democracy?,* pp. 101–02, 104–05; *Country Life Movement,* pp. 126–27; *Universal Service,* pp. 27–32. Bailey, "Country Living in the Next Generation," 337–38.

30. *Country Life Movement,* pp. 127–33, 12–13.

31. *What Is Democracy?,* pp. 64–65, 92–93; Bailey, *Ground–Levels in Democracy,* pp. 89–95.

32. Bailey to Gifford Pinchot, February 18, 1909, to Rev. S. W. Pratt, Campbell, New York, March 16, 1909, both in Bailey MSS; Bailey, *York State Rural Problems,* II, 138; Bailey, *Training of Farmers,* pp. 79–80; *Universal Service,* pp. 157–58.

33. Dorf, *Bailey,* pp. 191–92.

34. *Universal Service,* pp. 15–16; *Holy Earth,* pp. 87–88, 83, 78–79.

35. *Outlook to Nature,* pp. 178–82, 190–94; Bailey, "An Evolutionist's View of Nature and Religion"; *Training of Farmers,* p. 72; Dorf, *Bailey,* pp. 100–01; Rodgers, *Bailey,* pp. 349–50.

36. Dorf, *Bailey,* pp. 105–07; *Nature–Study Idea,* p. 137; Bailey, "Moon–Farming," 908–09.

37. *State and the Farmer,* pp. 57–60; *Country Life Movement,* pp. 183–87; *Holy Earth, passim.*

38. Bailey to C. P. Cary, Superintendent of Public Instruction, Madison, Wisconsin, January 25, 1909, Bailey MSS; Bailey, "Appeal to the Teachers"; *State and the Farmer,* p. 142; Bailey, "The New Education," 35.

39. "Appeal to the Teachers"; *Nature–Study Idea,* pp. 33–35,

54–60, 94–95, 108; "The New Education," 35; *Training of Farmers,* pp. 138–39, 143, 147; *State and the Farmer,* p. 142.

40. *Outlook to Nature,* pp. 118–19; *State and the Farmer,* pp. 139, 157; *Nature–Study Idea,* pp. 188, 89; "The New Education," 35; "Now the President Plans to Aid the Farmer"; *York State Rural Problems,* II, 221; Bailey, "School Gardens."

41. *Outlook to Nature,* pp. 173–74; Dorf, *Bailey,* pp. 110–12; Rodgers, *Bailey,* pp. 215–18, 236–37; *Nature–Study Idea,* pp. 5–6, 30–36, 50, 56. See Keppel, unpublished Ph.D. dissertation, Chapter III, for a discussion of Bailey and his nature study ideas.

42. *State and the Farmer,* p. 160; *Nature–Study Idea,* pp. 34–35; *Training of Farmers,* pp. 156, 151–52; Bailey, "Common Schools and the Farm Youth."

43. *Nature–Study Idea,* pp. 5–6, 50–57; Dorf, *Bailey,* p. 113; Rodgers, *Bailey,* p. 218; Bailey, "What This Magazine Stands For"; *Training of Farmers,* p. 151.

44. *Nature–Study Idea,* pp. 98–99, 106–07; *Outlook to Nature,* p. 80.

45. *Training of Farmers,* pp. 166–68, 171–72; *State and the Farmer,* pp. 106–09.

46. Bailey, "Place of Agriculture in Higher Education," 253–54; Kern, "Consolidated School and the New Agriculture," p. 278; *Outlook to Nature,* pp. 100, 102–03; Dorf, *Bailey,* pp. 195–97; Lawrence, "Bailey," 31.

47. *State and the Farmer,* pp. 135–36, 170; *Country Life Movement,* pp. 75–76; Bailey, "State Program for Rural Betterment," pp. 41–42; *York State Rural Problems,* II, 54–56.

48. Dewey, *School and Society, passim;* Dewey, "School As a Social Center," pp. 379–80; Dewey, *My Pedogogic Creed, passim; Nature–Study Idea,* pp. 94–95; Dorf, *Bailey,* p. 104; *Outlook to Nature,* p. 103; *State and the Farmer,* pp. 137–38; Keppel, unpublished Ph.D. dissertation, pp. 202–08.

CHAPTER FIVE

1. *Report, Country Life Comm.,* pp. 20–22, 28–47. Shortly after its limited initial publication as a government document, the *Report* was published by the Spokane, Washington, Chamber of Commerce. The Sturgis and Walton Company of New York published it in 1911 and again in 1917. The most recent publication of the *Report* was by the University of North Carolina Press in 1944.

2. *Ibid.,* pp. 28–47.

3. *Ibid.*

4. *Ibid.,* pp. 48–65.

5. *Ibid.,* p. 50. For statements supporting these last two contentions, see Plunkett, *Rural Life Problem of the United States,* p. 31; and Rodgers, *Bailey,* p. 366.

6. Ellsworth, "Theodore Roosevelt's Country Life Commission," 171.

7. Bailey, *Training of Farmers,* p. 3.

8. Gill and Pinchot, *Country Church,* pp. 3–4; Kinley, "Movement of Population," 118; Edward A. Ross, "Folk Depletion as a Cause of Rural Decline," 26–27; "Birth-Control and Race-Suicide," 244–45.

9. Zimmerman, "Migration to Towns and Cities," *American Journal of Sociology,* XXXII, 105–09, XXXIII, 237–41; Zimmerman and Smith, "Migration to Towns and Cities"; Gee, "A Qualitative Study of Rural Depopulation"; 210–21; Gee and Runk, "Qualitative Selection in Cityward Migration."

10. See, for example, "Malthusian Theory"; Trimble, "Influence of the Passing of the Public Lands"; Thompson, *Population: A Study of Malthusianism,* pp. 131, 145, 162–63; F. Vrooman, "Uncle Sam's Romance With Science and the Soil"; "Expansion By Irrigation."

11. G. Holmes, "Movement from City and Town to Farms"; Stowe, "Training City Boys for Country Life"; "Farmer Colonies for Land Hungry"; Sherwood, "Taking Thought for American Agriculture"; Phelps, "Coming Exodus."

12. For discussions of back-to-the-land movements in Europe, see "Hobbling Back to Nature"; Haggard, "Back to the Land"; Mosse, "Mystical Origins of National Socialism."

13. Bailey, *Country Life Movement,* pp. 1–2; Bailey, *York State Rural Problems,* II, 118–19; "Hobbling Back to Nature"; *Report, Country Life Comm.* p. 29; Plunkett, *Rural Life Problem of the United States,* pp. 152–53.

14. Bailey, *York State Rural Problems,* II, 129–32; Carver, "The Work of Rural Organization," 822. Between February, 1912 and March, 1914, *World's Work* ran an article devoted to farm information in each issue.

15. For evidence of some success in colonizing efforts, see "Hobbling Back to Nature"; Sherwood, "Taking Thought for American Agriculture"; "Farmer Colonies for Land Hungry."

16. This is not to deny that some farms were lying idle. In commercialized agriculture, some farmers were forced out through their use of poor farming practices, just as some of the farm population was forced off the land by technological change, but these hardly justified the great concern which was then being expressed.

17. Bailey, *York State Rural Problems,* II, 111–12, 114–15, 199–201; Bailey, *State and the Farmer,* pp. 22–54; Bailey to Ray Stannard Baker, October 10, 1910, Series 2, Box 93, Baker MSS.

18. Ghent, *Our Benevolent Feudalism,* p. 50; "Our Farmers Move Often"; Roosevelt, *Wallaces' Farmer,* XXXII (October 11, 1907), 1145, cited in Saloutos and Hicks, *Agricultural Discontent,* p. 14; Joseph Ross, "Agrarian Revolution," 382–89. Ross saw this last development taking place only two years after the Roosevelt statement.

19. The "agricultural ladder" thesis has been challenged but not vitiated by Lawanda F. Cox in her article, "Tenancy in the United States." Mrs. Cox cites the migration of rural wage-earners to seek

jobs in industry during the 1880s and 1890s as suggestive of a situation in agriculture where opportunity for advancement was closed. However, this fails to take into account the sociological truism that position in the urban status system is considered superior to position in the rural system. Therefore, if status were a consideration—and there is evidence that it often was—the migration of people from rural areas to the cities would be irrelevant to the absence of an agricultural mobility pattern.

20. Hibbard, "Farm Tenancy in the United States", 29; Spillman, "Agricultural Ladder," 178; *Report, Country Life Comm.*, p. 45.

21. J. Ross, "Agrarian Revolution," 382–89; Eastman, "Rural Churches That Do Their Job," 586; Henry Wallace to Walter Hines Page, March 13, 1913, Wallace MSS; Hibbard, "Compensating Tenants for Improvements." Hibbard proposed that the length of time of farm leases be extended so that tenants could recover their investment in improvements.

22. For support of the conclusion that many landlords of the period were speculators see Hibbard, "Farm Tenancy in the United States," 38.

23. Rossiter, "Decrease in Rural Population," 80. Rossiter was a writer, publisher, one-time government statistician, and friend of Theodore Roosevelt.

24. "Farmer's Problems," 645; "Farm Labor Problem"; *Report, Country Life Comm.* pp. 41–44.

25. Rumely, "Passing of the Man With the Hoe"; Vance, "Why Young Men Leave the Farm."

26. "Agriculture the True Source of Our Wealth"; "Farmer's Problems," 645; "Farm Immigrants"; Hays, "Relations of Farmer and Factory Worker."

27. Roberts, "Farmer and His Profits"; Warren Wilson, "Farm Cooperation," 51.

28. For examples of such statements, see *Report, Country Life Comm.*, pp. 21–22.

29. The feeling that farming had to be made more profitable was widespread. See the following for examples of some who used the theme: "Farmers and the Future," 9847; Taylor, "From Plowed Land to Pavement," 24–25; Carver, "Work of Rural Organization," 823; I. Roberts, "Farmer and His Profits."

30. Carney, *Country Life and the Country School*, pp. 323–24.

31. Roosevelt, "Welfare of the Farmers"; *Report, Country Life Comm.*, pp. 15, 37; Malin, "Background of First Bills to Establish a Bureau of Markets"; Hofstadter, *Age of Reform*, p. 112.

32. Hofstadter, *Age of Reform*, p. 113, indicates that 10,701 of 10,803 marketing and purchasing organizations listed in 1925 were formed after 1890.

33. Eyerly, "Co-operative Movements Among Farmers," 67; Buck, *Granger Movement*, pp. 259–67.

34. See, for example, "More Money for the Farmer."

35. Van Cortland, "What Is Agricultural Credit?"; Carver, "Work of Rural Organization," 826–31.

36. The literature on the rural credit system is voluminous. See, for example, Bailey, "Wise Words on Rural Credits"; "Credit for Farmers"; Ousley, "Beginnings of Rural Credit," 511–12; "Cheaper Money for the Farmer"; Collins, "Will the Rural Credits Law Work?", 791.

37. Meyer, "Postal Savings Banks"; Carter, "Postal Savings Banks"; "Postal Savings"; "It Must Come," 986.

38. "Parcels Post"; Fuller, *RFD,* pp. 199–227; Emmet and Jeuck, *Catalogues and Counters,* pp. 191–92.

39. *Report, Country Life Comm.,* p. 38. The need for improved education, discussed below, was the other most commonly mentioned deficiency.

40. Fuller, *RFD,* pp. 177–98; Parker, "Good Roads Movement"; "For Good Roads"; Davis, "Iowa Farm Opinion and the Good Roads Movement," 324–25.

41. Carney, *Country Life and the Country School,* pp. 114, 117–19; B. F. Harris to Edmund James, November 17, 1915, Box 87, James MSS; Liberty Hyde Bailey to Theodore Roosevelt, July 6, 1914, Series 1, Box 268, Roosevelt MSS; *Report, Country Life Comm.,* p. 38.

42. Carney, *Country Life and the Country School,* pp. 114–19; Parker, "Good Roads Movement."

43. The universality of these charges makes complete citation impractical; several representative sources are: Foght, "The Country School"; Carney, *Country Life and the Country School,* pp. 139–44; "Farmers and the Future." It was admitted on occasion that even a rural education stressed certain widely accepted ideals. No one suggested, for example, that McGuffey's *Reader,* with its stories emphasizing thrift, honesty, virtue, loyalty, and patriotism, be thrown out.

44. Kemp, "Statement on Work, Purposes, Etc. of the Country Life Commission."

45. Foght, "Country School," 153; Monahan, "Development of Rural School a Problem of Tremendous Importance"; Hill, "Little Red Schoolhouse a 'Fake,'" 317–18; Betts, *New Ideals in Rural Schools,* p. 19.

46. "National Conference on Rural Education and Rural Life," 390.

47. Foght, "Country School," 153–54; Betts, *New Ideals in Rural Schools,* p. 25; Amelia Shaw MacDonald, Delhi, New York, to Bailey, October 16, 1918, Bailey MSS.

48. Foght, "Country School," 157; "Rural Life and Education," 1632; "Country School," 883; Poe, "Farmer Children Need Farmer Studies," 3761; Bailey, *Nature–Study Idea,* pp. 5ff.; Bailey, *Training of Farmers,* pp. 138–39, 143, 147; Bailey, *State and the Farmer,* p. 142. Some advocates of the school-garden idea even suggested the rebuilding of rural schools on plots of one to twenty-five acres so that pupils would be able to have individual garden areas.

49. Poe, "Farmer Children Need Farmer Studies," 3761; B. F. Harris to Edmund James, February 26, 1912, Box 27, James MSS; Crosby, "How May the Rural Schools Be More Closely Related to the Life and Needs of the People," pp. 969–70. One reformer even be-

lieved that it would not be out of place for the new country school to teach eugenics.

50. "Country School," 882.

51. Foght, "Country School," 151; "Teaching the Teachers."

52. Carney, *Country Life and the Country School,* p. 187.

53. Ellsworth, "Coming of Rural Consolidated Schools," 121–22; "Consolidation of Rural Schools," 579; Dille, "Reorganization of the Country School," pp. 302–03; Grupe, "How Problems of the Rural Schools Are Being Met," 484–85. An exception to the view of consolidation generally held by reformers was Liberty Hyde Bailey's opinion that ineffective one-room schools should be salvaged because they were "schools of the people" and closer to farm life conditions than larger units located in a town or village. While there is some merit in Bailey's plea, one suspects that it was motivated largely by nostalgia and sentiment. See Bailey, *State and the Farmer,* p. 141; *York State Rural Problems,* II, 217–18; *Training of Farmers,* p. 156.

54. See, for example, Carney, *Country Life and the Country School,* pp. 43–49; Cubberly, *Rural Life and Education,* pp. 77–81; Gill and Pinchot, *Country Church;* Butterfield, *Country Church and the Rural Problem;* Wilson, *Church of the Open Country;* W. Wilson, "Church and the Rural Community"; Wells, "Country Church and Its Social Problem"; Bricker, *Solving the Country Church Problem,* pp. 51–55.

55. W. Wilson, "Social Life in the Country," 126; W. Wilson, "Church and the Rural Community," 678–79; "Country Church"; Fiske, *Challenge of the Country,* p. 125; Bricker, *Solving the Country Church Problem,* pp. 78–79.

56. Carney, *Country Life and the Country School,* p. 43; Bricker, *Solving the Country Church Problem,* p. 55; Wells, "Country Church," 297–303.

57. Eastman, "Rural Churches That Do Their Job"; Wilson, *Church of the Open Country,* pp. 4–16.

58. Wilson, *Church of the Open Country,* p. 74; "Country Life Commission and the Church." 490; Gill and Pinchot, *Country Church,* pp. 42–46; Deiman, "Institutional Church for the Rural Community."

59. "Problems of the Country Church"; "Theology and Country Life"; Bramhall, "Back to the Soil Movement in California"; Wilson, *Church of the Open Country,* pp. 63–64; Gill and Pinchot, *Country Church,* pp. 46–50.

60. Bricker, *Solving the Country Church Problem,* p. 122.

61. Gill and Pinchot, *Country Church,* pp. 28–33; Bricker, *Solving the Country Church Problem,* pp. 79–81; Carney, *Country Life and the Country School,* p. 49; *Report, Country Life Comm.,* pp. 61–62.

CHAPTER SIX

1. Ellsworth, "Theodore Roosevelt's Country Life Commission," 158; Bailey, *State and the Farmer,* pp. 88–94; Bailey, *York State Rural Problems,* I, 239; Cornell University Agricultural Experiment

Station, *An Agricultural Survey; Report, Country Life Comm.*, pp. 19, 52–53.

2. Brunner, *Growth of a Science*, pp. 4, 7, 8; Wilson, *Quaker Hill;* Gill and Pinchot, *Country Church;* Galpin, "Development of the Science and Philosophy of American Rural Society," 202–03. Gill and Pinchot were cousins.

3. Brunner, *Growth of a Science*, p. 8.

4. Carney, *Country Life and the Country School*, pp. 54–56; "Great Country Life Movement," 617; "Equipment of Some Michigan County Schools."

5. "Rural Life and Education," 1631; Carney, *Country Life and the Country School*, 323–24; S. Knapp, "An Agricultural Revolution."

6. U.S. Dept. Agr., *History of Agricultural Extension Work*, pp. 42–73; McConnell, *Decline of Agrarian Democracy*, pp. 20–29.

7. U.S. Dept. Agr., *History of Agricultural Extension Work*, pp. 58ff.; McConnell, *Decline of Agrarian Democracy*, pp. 23–25; J. Bailey, *Knapp;* Cline, *Knapp*, pp. 51–57, 64–69.

8. U.S. Dept. Agr., *History of Agricultural Extension Work*, pp. 100–15.

9. *Ibid.*, pp. 35–41; U.S. Dept. Agr., *Farmers' Institutes and Agricultural Extension Work;* U.S. Dept. Agr., *Farmers' Institutes for Women.*

10. S. Knapp, "Farmers' Cooperative Demonstration Work," p. 160; S. Knapp, "Agricultural Education," p. 954; J. Bailey, *Knapp*, pp. 213–14, 233–37.

11. Association of American Agricultural Colleges and Experiment Stations, Twenty-second Annual Convention, *Proceedings, 1915*, pp. 49, 68–69, 232–41; McConnell, *Decline of Agrarian Democracy*, pp. 48–50.

12. U.S. Dept. Agr., *History of Agricultural Extension Work*, pp. 180, 185; Burritt, *County Agent and the Farm Bureau*, pp. 153–63.

13. See the early chapters of McConnell, *Decline of Agrarian Democracy*, for a documented account of the "capture" of the extension movement by the Farm Bureau. See also Burritt, *County Agent and the Farm Bureau*, pp. 210–14.

14. Letters from farmers in the Bailey MSS collection support this conclusion. See, for example, R. R. Smith, RFD 1, Wayne, Nebraska, to Henry Wallace, September 8, 1908; John Masters, RFD 4, Jacksonville, Florida, to Bailey, December 4, 1908; J. W. Spencer to Bailey, n.d.; and Matthew Jansen, Maize, Kansas, to Theodore Roosevelt, January 23, 1909.

15. Carney, *Country Life and the Country School*, p. 309; "Social Problems of the Farmer"; Kates, "Origin and Growth of Rural Conferences," 112–15; *Report, Country Life Comm.* pp. 52–53.

16. "Rural Life Conference"; "Great Country Life Movement," 618; *First Wisconsin Country Life Conference* (Bulletin of the University of Wisconsin); *Daily Chronicle* (DeKalb, Illinois), July 31, 1912, pp. 1–2; G. L. Brown, Acting President, South Dakota State College, Brookings, to Benjamin H. Hibbard, January 29, 1914, File Box 2, Hibbard MSS; "Louisville Convention for Rural Betterment."

17. "Cities and the Farm Movement"; "Interstate Agricultural Congress."

18. "Great Country Life Movement."

19. "New England Conference to Promote Rural Progress."

20. "What the Country School Must Be."

21. "Rural Uplift in the Southwest."

22. "National Conference on Rural Education at the University of Pennsylvania."

23. Carney, *Country Life and the Country School,* p. 53; Bramhall, "Back to the Soil Movement in California."

24. Morse, "Marketing and Farm Credits"; "Banker–Farmer Alliance for Cooperation"; Eugene Davenport, "Relation of the Bankers to Agricultural Progress," typescript of speech before Illinois Bankers' Association, October 11, 1911, Box 6, Davenport MSS; Davenport, "Bankers in Agriculture," typescript, September 8, 1913, Box 7, Davenport MSS.

25. "Great Country Life Movement," 618; "Conference on Rural Life"; A. R. Mann to Theodore Roosevelt, May 29, 1913, Series 1, Box 251, Roosevelt MSS; "Community Engineer vs. Community Leader"; "School for Rural Social Workers"; "Rural Leaders on Their Problems."

26. Kates, "Origin and Growth of Rural Conferences," 116; "Great Country Life Movement," 618; *Wallaces' Farmer,* XXXVI (April 21, 1911), 716–17; *ibid.,* (August 25, 1911), 1163.

27. Carney, *Country Life and the Country School,* pp. 310, 316–18; Butterfield, "Can Rural Social Forces Be Federated?", 456; Butterfield, *Chapters in Rural Progress,* pp. 233–51; Wells, "Is An Organized Country Life Movement Possible?", 451–56; "New England Conference to Promote Rural Progress"; *Daily Chronicle* (DeKalb, Illinois), July 31, 1912, pp. 1–2.

28. Sanderson, "Country–Life Forces Mobilizing"; National Country Life Association, *Proceedings of the First National Country Life Conference, 1919.*

29. Sanderson, "Country–Life Forces Mobilizing"; *Proceedings of the First National Country Life Conference, 1919.*

30. *Report, Country Life Comm.,* p. 16.

31. The notes and bibliography of this study provide a part of the documentation here. The *Reader's Guide to Periodical Literature* and the *Agricultural Index* for these years indicate literally hundreds of articles on rural problems.

32. See, for example, J. W. Spencer to Bailey, n.d.; John Masters, RFD 4, Jacksonville, Florida, to Bailey, December 4, 1908; "A Republican" (farmer) to Country Life Commission, November 28, 1908 —all in the Bailey MSS; "A St. Lawrence County Farmer"; Fiske, *Challenge of the Country,* p. 19; "Farm Commission"; "Plutocratic Farmer."

33. Stone to Norval Kemp, secretary to the Country Life Commission, November 20, 1908, Bailey MSS.

34. "A St. Lawrence County Farmer"; "Country Life Problems," 479; "What Do the Farmers Want?"; "Wrong Remedy"; "Our Wash-

ington Letter"; Peer, "What Is the Matter With Agriculture?"

35. *National Stockman and Farmer*, XXXII (October 22, 1908).

36. "Editor's Diary," 569; "Paternalism"; *Journal of Commerce* (New York), quoted in "Presidential Anxiety for the Farmer," 235; editorial comment in "Hardware Section"; Miller, "Why Farmers Must Work Together."

37. "Country Life Problems," 479; "Country vs. City"; Strong, *Challenge of the City,* pp. 30–31; R. Holmes, "Passing of the Farmer," 523; "Farm and City."

38. Bill, "What's the Matter With the Farmer?"; "President's Concern"; H. E. Stockbridge, editor, *Southern Ruralist* (Atlanta), to Theodore Roosevelt, September 15, 1908, Bailey MSS; editorial, *Spokesman–Review* (Spokane, Washington), August 12, 1908; "Will Farmers Help Themselves?"

39. *Report, Country Life Comm.*, p. 44.

40. All of these were actual recommendations of the Country Life Commission. See *ibid.*, pp. 15–16, 36–37, 41, 46, 53–56.

41. Benedict, *Farm Policies of the United States,* pp. 126–28, 129–33, 139–51; *Report, Country Life Comm.*, p. 45; Hofstadter, *Age of Reform*, pp. 118–19.

42. Benedict, *Farm Policies of the United States,* pp. 126–28, 129–33, 139–51, 184; Hofstadter, *Age of Reform*, pp. 118–19; Nourse, *Legal Status of Agricultural Co-operation,* pp. 252–61.

CHAPTER SEVEN

1. G. Wendell Bush, Arden, New York, to Bailey, December 17, 1908, Bailey MSS. Some farmer letters addressed to Theodore Roosevelt and similar to those in the Bailey MSS are in Boxes 1742–1743 of the Pinchott MSS.

2. "A St. Lawrence County Farmer."

3. Matthew Jansen, Maize, Kansas, to Theodore Roosevelt, January 23, 1909, Bailey MSS.

4. "A St. Lawrence County Farmer."

5. Comstock, "Nature–Study and Agriculture."

6. J. W. Spencer, no place of origin given, to Bailey, n.d., Bailey MSS.

7. See, for example, "Prefer to Uplift Themselves"; Bell, "From the Man Who Holds the Plow," 828; "Farm Women Find Life Hard," Part V, p. 15; Vontrees, "A Farmer Speaks," 292; Rodgers, *Bailey,* p. 365.

8. *Prairie Farmer*, June 15, 1913, cited in Johnstone, "Old Ideals Versus New Ideas in Farm Life," p. 154.

9. "Will Farmers Help Themselves?"

10. Carney, *Country Life and the Country School,* pp. 101–02, 128.

11. Address before the forty-second session of the National Grange, Washington, D. C., November 11, 1908, quoted in Atkeson,

Semi–Centennial History of the Patrons of Husbandry, pp. 255–57.

12. *National Grange Monthly,* December, 1913, p. 17, cited in Benedict, *Farm Policies of the United States,* p. 158.

13. Bell, "From the Man Who Holds the Plow," 828–29.

14. Francis Rawle, Montgomery County, Pennsylvania, to Bailey, October 14, 1908, Bailey MSS.

15. Quoted in Saloutos and Hicks, *Agricultural Discontent,* pp. 128–29.

16. *Ibid.;* Bailey, "Why Do the Boys Leave the Farm?"; Bailey, "Why Do Some Boys Take to Farming?"

17. Clipping, "Late Meeting of York State Fruit Growers," *Daily Enterprise* (Burlington, New Jersey), August 21, 1908, in Bailey MSS. See also the letters from farmers and Country Life Commission circulars in the Bailey, Pinchot, and Butterfield MSS.

18. See, for example, John Masters, RFD 4, Jacksonville, Florida, to Bailey, December 4, 1908, Bailey MSS; "A Republican" (farmer), no place of origin given, to the commission, November 28, 1908, Bailey MSS; Rodgers, *Bailey,* p. 265.

19. "Prefer to Uplift Themselves."

20. Peer, "What Is the Matter With Agriculture?"; *Maine Farmer* (Augusta), *Farm and Fireside* (Springfield, Ohio), cited in "Farm Papers on Rural Uplift"; editorial, *National Stockman and Farmer,* XXXII (October 22, 1908).

21. "Paternalism"; Parsons, "Henry Wallace's Estimate of Dry Land Farming," 5.

22. *Farm, Stock and Home* (Minneapolis), cited in "Farm Papers on Rural Uplift"; "Our Washington Letter"; "Milk and Water"; "Country Life Commission, How Much Did It Accomplish?", 231.

23. "Milk and Water"; "Country Life Commission, How Much Did It Accomplish?"

24. Carney, *Country Life and the Country School,* pp. 171–75.

25. Ellsworth, "Coming of Rural Consolidated Schools," 123–24, Henry Wallace to Theodore Roosevelt, August 31, 1910, Series 1, Box 149, Roosevelt MSS. The costs of consolidated schools were admittedly higher than under the older system but reformers argued that farmers were spending too little on their schools.

26. Ellsworth, "Coming of Rural Consolidated Schools," 123–24; Carney, *Country Life and the Country School,* pp. 171–75; Betts, *New Ideals in Rural Schools,* pp. 37–38; Mitchell, "American Farm Woman as She Sees Herself," p. 316; True, "Some Problems of the Rural Common School," pp. 144–45.

27. Ernest Ingersoll, "Memorandum of Contents of Reports of Farmers' Meetings," n.d., Bailey MSS. Ingersoll was the special agent of the Census Bureau who did the tabulating for the commission.

28. Ernest Ingersoll, "Report Upon Answers to Circulars With Suggestions for Utilizing the Information," December 21, 1908, Bailey MSS.

29. This view was widely held, and the following are cited as representative: U.S. Dept. Agr., *Social and Labor Needs of Farm*

Women, p. 22; Bell, "From the Man Who Holds the Plow," 826; and in the Bailey MSS, Mrs. A. Tompkins, Riddle, Oregon, to Bailey, November 17, 1908; F. E. Baxter, Toswell, Idaho, Country Life Commission circular; J. H. Hudgins, Denison, Texas, Country Life Commission circular; P. J. Jewett, RFD 8, Butler, Missouri, to Henry Wallace, August 24, 1908; Harry B. Warner, Angelica, New York, to the commission, November 5, 1908.

30. See, for example, Bell, "From the Man Who Holds the Plow," 826.

31. *Ibid.*

32. Complete documentation of this position is manifold, and the following are cited as a representative sample: Bell, "From the Man Who Holds the Plow," 826, and, from the Bailey MSS, J. R. Molloy, Pottsboro, Texas, Country Life Commission circular; E. H. Temple, LaFayette County, Missouri, to Henry Wallace, October 26, 1908; Harry B. Warner, Angelica, New York, to the commission, November 5, 1908; J. G. Fargo, Batavia, New York, to Bailey, December 10, 1908; W. E. Kapp, "Report of Frenchman Hill District 185, School–House Meeting," Douglas County, Washington, December 3, 1908.

33. S. T. Barnes, Sherman, Texas, circular, Bailey MSS.

34. N. R. Taylor, RFD 2, Bardwell, Kentucky, to Bailey, December 1, 1908, Bailey MSS; Resolution of Genesee County Grange, submitted with letter from J. G. Fargo, Batavia, New York, to Bailey, December 10, 1908, Bailey MSS.

35. E. A. Allbee, Montpelier, Iowa, to Henry Wallace, August 29, 1908, Bailey MSS; J. R. Molloy, Country Life Commission circular, Bailey MSS.

36. E. H. Temple to Henry Wallace, October 26, 1908, Bailey MSS.

37. Halstead, "Automatic Farm."

38. Hays, *Response to Industrialism,* p. 113; J. Bailey, *Knapp,* p. 178.

39. See, for example, Bell, "From the Man Who Holds the Plow," 827–28.

40. *Report, Country Life Comm.,* pp. 38, 53; Ingersoll, "Memorandum of Contents of Reports of Farmers' Meetings"; J. C. Spees, Country Life Commission circular, October 26, 1908; "A Republican," November 28, 1908, Bailey MSS. Actually, the commission received no appropriation for its work—the request was voted down. It did, however, receive $5,000 privately from the Russell Sage Foundation. See John M. Glenn, secretary and director, Russell Sage Foundation, to Bailey, October 28, 1908, Bailey MSS.

41. Greathouse, "Free Delivery of Rural Mails," pp. 523–26; Shelby, "Open Letter to Secretary Houston from a Farmer's Wife," 925.

42. R. A. Sullivan, Arcade, New York, to Bailey, November 17, 1908, Bailey MSS.

43. Saloutos and Hicks, *Agricultural Discontent,* p. 26; letters-to-the-editor, *Wallaces' Farmer,* January 29, 1904, February 12, 1904,

February 19, 1904, all cited in Davis, "Iowa Farm Opinion and the Good Roads Movement," 333.

44. "Hawkeye Subscriber," *The Homestead* (Des Moines), December 17, 1903, p. 13 (885), cited in Davis, "Iowa Farm Opinion and the Good Roads Movement," 333–34. Page numbers for *The Homestead* indicate the page in a given issue and cumulative page number (in parentheses) for the volume.

45. *The Homestead* (Des Moines), June 25, 1903, Farmers' Institute Edition, p. 7 (91), *Wallaces' Farmer*, June 26, 1903, p. 908, both cited in Davis, "Iowa Farm Opinion and the Good Roads Movement," 332.

46. Unidentified tabulation, Bailey MSS. Many of the returned questionnaires for this phase of the Country Life Commission's investigation are in the Butterfield MSS.

47. Carney, *Country Life and the Country School*, p. 43.

48. Bricker, *Solving the Country Church Problem*, pp. 79–81.

49. Anton T. Boisen, "Factors Which Have to Do With the Decline of the Country Church." John M. Gillette noted in 1917 that the rural churches of North Dakota had changed little during the preceding decade, for they continued to preach personal salvation and ignore the social situation. See Gillette to A. J. Todd, April 23, 1917, Box 1, Gillette MSS.

50. Page to Henry Wallace, August 14, 1912 and August 19, 1912, Box 1, Folder 12, Wallace MSS.

51. Boisen, "Factors Which Have to Do With the Decline of the Country Church," 183–84. Boisen also concluded that tenancy as a factor in church deterioration was overstated, since in a state such as Maine where there were few tenants, there was also little interest in the church. See *ibid.*, 182–83.

52. Ingersoll, "Report Upon Answers to the Circulars"; *Report, Country Life Comm.*, pp. 35–36.

53. See, for example, "A St. Lawrence County Farmer"; Bell, "From the Man Who Holds the Plow," 826–27; and, in the Bailey MSS, R. R. Smith, RFD 1, Wayne, Nebraska, to Wallace, September 8, 1908; Alexander Bicksler, RFD 4, Los Angeles, to Bailey, December 6, 1908; F. A. Seeley, Canandaigua, New York, to Bailey, December 3, 1908; John Masters to Bailey, December 4, 1908; Harry B. Warner to commission, November 5, 1908; Matthew Jansen to Theodore Roosevelt, January 23, 1909.

54. *Report, Country Life Comm.*, p. 35.

55. Ingersoll, "Report Upon Answers to the Circulars."

56. *Ibid.*

57. See, for example, in the Bailey MSS: Alexander Bicksler to Bailey, December 6, 1908; Kapp, "Report, Frenchman Hill District 185 School–House Meeting," December 3, 1908; A. H. Weeks, A. C. Rubeck, and George Cross, "Report of School–House Meeting, Valleyford, Washington," December 9, 1908; S. W. Calhoun, RFD 3, Fayetteville, Arkansas, to Bailey, December 8, 1908; J. C. Leonard, Cedar Rapids, Iowa, January 9, 1909; and G. W. Van Hooser, Auburn, California, January 10, 1909, to editor, *American Farm Review,*

(Rochester, New York). The *American Farm Review* urged farmers to respond to the Country Life Commission circular and therefore received some letters and circulars which it forwarded to Bailey.

58. Bell, "From the Man Who Holds the Plow," 826–27; Harry B. Warner, to commission, November 5, 1908, Bailey MSS; Alexander Bicksler to Bailey, December 6, 1908, Bailey MSS. The farmers' market idea took hold and many were established throughout the country during the years just prior to and during the First World War. The vestiges of some of these, usually the name, still survive today.

59. "A St. Lawrence County Farmer"; letter-to-the-editor from a farm reader, *Wallaces' Farmer*, XXXVII (November 25, 1912), 1602; and, in the Bailey MSS, Matthew Jansen to Theodore Roosevelt, January 23, 1909; John Masters to Bailey, December 3, 1908; F. A. Seeley to Bailey, December 3, 1908; John S. Stevenson, Box 52, Helena, Montana, to Bailey, December 3, 1908.

60. Ingersoll, "Report Upon Answers to the Circulars"; Plunkett, *Rural Life Problem of the United States,* pp. 94–95; Voorhies, *American Cooperatives,* pp. 81–83; Hofstadter, *Age of Reform,* p. 113.

61. Ingersoll, "Report Upon Answers to the Circulars," Inquiry X, "Have the farmers in your neighborhood satisfactory facilities for business in banking, credit, insurance, etc.?"

62. Interestingly, a summary of comments on rural credits by the agricultural press in 1914 indicated that nearly seventy percent of the seventy-four journals included favored some sort of farm credit facility. There was, however, wide disagreement as to the details. See "References in the Agricultural Press Regarding the Fletcher–Moss Land Bank Bill," Secretary of Agriculture, General Correspondence, NA, RG 16.

63. Ingersoll, "Memorandum of Contents of Reports of Farmers' Meetings," Bailey MSS.

64. Ingersoll, "Report Upon Answers to the Circulars."

65. Cover letter accompanying "Memorandum of Contents of Reports," A. C. True, Director of the Office of Experiment Stations, to Bailey, January 6, 1909, Bailey MSS.

66. Nelson, "Farmers on Farm Life," 78–79.

67. Letters in the Bailey MSS include: Otto P. Mason, Wichita, Kansas, to Bailey, October 18, 1908; G. B. Cramer, RFD 16, Milton, Indiana, to Bailey, August 31, 1908; G. B. Cramer to Pinchot, September 6, 1908; G. C. Buck, Shannon, Kansas, to the commission, n.d.; Buck to Norval Kemp, secretary to the commission, December 21, 1908.

68. For reference to the letter, see W. C. Haymond, Francesville, Indiana, to Roosevelt, November 16, 1908, Box 1742, Pinchot MSS.

69. Cramer to Bailey, August 31, 1908; Cramer to Pinchot, September 6, 1908, Bailey MSS.

70. Buck to Country Life Commission, n.d.; Buck to Kemp, December 21, 1908, Bailey MSS. A copy of Kemp's letter to Buck was not found, but its contents were inferred from Buck's reply in December. Ironically, the Country Life Commission included a suggestion in its report which was similar to Buck's proposal that schools to train

farm workers be established. See *Report, Country Life Comm.* p. 45.

71. *Report, Country Life Comm.*, pp. 46–47; "Farm Women Find Life Hard," Part V, p. 15; U.S. Dept. Agr., *Social and Labor Needs of Farm Women;* Nelson, "Farmers on Farm Life," 78–79.

72. "Farm Women Find Life Hard."

73. *Ibid.*

74. "Farm Wives Tell of Further Needs."

75. See, for example, C. W. Walter, Labaddie, Missouri, to Bailey November 17, 1908, Bailey MSS; R. R. Smith to Henry Wallace, September 8, 1908, Bailey MSS; Halstead, "Automatic Farm"; Pearse, "How to Keep Young Folks on the Farms."

76. "Farm Women Find Life Hard," Part V, p. 15.

77. Letter from an Illinois subscriber, *Wallaces' Farmer*, XXXIV (January 15, 1909), 68.

78. *Ibid.*

79. *Report, Country Life Comm.*, p. 44; Farmer's Wife, "The Child and the Farm"; Cook, "Letter from a Farmer's Wife."

80. R. R. Smith to Henry Wallace, September 8, 1908, Bailey MSS; Johnstone, "Old Ideals Versus New Ideas in Farm Life," pp. 146–47.

81. Ingersoll, "Report Upon Answers to Circulars."

82. See, in the Bailey MSS: L. W. Swanzey, Ridott, Illinois, to Bailey, August 16, 1908; Ura Embry, Sherman, Texas, Country Life Commission circular; P. J. Jewett to Wallace, August 24, 1908; E. H. Temple to Wallace, October 26, 1908; Kapp, "Report of Frenchman Hill District 185 School–House Meeting," December 3, 1908; Weeks, *et. al.*, "Report of School–House Meeting, Valleyford, Washington," December 9, 1908; A. N. Somers, "Report of Mass Meeting on Country Life Questions," Montague, Massachusetts, December 5, 1908.

83. Unidentified tabulation of responses to special questions sent out by the Country Life Commission, covering the topics of farmers' organizations, the recreative and social life of the people, moral conditions of country life, and the country church, n.d., Bailey MSS. A similar tabulation is in the Butterfield MSS.

84. "Teaching the Farmer to Play," 308.

85. E. A. Allbee, RFD 1, Montpelier, Iowa, to Wallace, August 29, 1908; Mrs. H. B. Rose, Middlefield, Ohio, to Theodore Roosevelt, September 5, 1908; Mrs. Rose to Norval Kemp, October 22, 1908, all in the Bailey MSS.

86. Ingersoll, "Report Upon Answers to Circulars."

87. Letter, J. P. Brown, Chenango, New York, to Board of Health, New York City, enclosed as a clipping with letter-to-the-editor, C. L. Wooley, n.d., to *Country Gentleman*, LXXIV (May 6, 1909), 459–60; "New Era for Farm Women," *Good Housekeeping*, XLIX (July, 1909), 39–43. *Good Housekeeping* magazine had its own "National Farm Home Inquiry," in 1909.

88. Shelby, "Open Letter to Secretary Houston from a Farmer's Wife," 924–25. In the Bailey MSS: E. E. Bailey, Denison, Texas,

Country Life Commission circular; Mrs. H. B. Rose to Norval Kemp, October 22, 1908; S. T. Barnes, Sherman, Texas, Country Life Commission circular; Mrs. Anna Thomas, RFD 3, Bainbridge, Indiana, to Bailey, November 15, 1908.

89. Ingersoll, "Report Upon Answers to Circulars." See also, Harvey W. Wiley, "Rural Sanitation," typescript dated 1910, Box 191, Wiley MSS.

90. "Remarkable Study of a Rural Community," 264.

91. "Some Solid Reasons for a Strike of Farm Wives."

92. "Why Young Women Are Leaving Our Farms," 56.

CHAPTER EIGHT

1. Weeks, "The Question of Agricultural Population," 255.

2. Even ignoring the impact of industrialization, some rural people had to leave the farms since retaining all of them would soon result in overpopulation of country districts due to the fact that rural America produced more people than it lost through deaths and retirement.

3. See Clarence Ousley, speech before the 1915 convention of the Association of American Agricultural Colleges and Experiment Stations, cited in McConnell, *Decline of Agrarian Democracy*, p. 49.

4. See, for example, *Report, Country Life Comm.*, pp. 36–38, 56.

5. "Waste Land."

Appendix:

Country Life Leadership Sample

Name	Occupation or Position	Association with Movement
Bailey, Liberty H.	Dir., State Ag. Coll. (N.Y.)	Member, Country Life Comm.; books; articles; confs.
Barrett, Charles S.	Pres., Farmers' Union	Member, Country Life Comm.; confs.
Benson, Oscar H.	Co. supt. of schools	Boys-girls extension work; books; articles
Betts, George H.	Prof., psych.	Book on rural schools; confs.
Bralley, Francis M.	State Supt. of Pub. Instruc. (Tex.)	Confs.; pamphlets
Bricker, Garland A.	Educator	Books on rural sch.; editor, *Rural Educator;* confs.
Brittain, Marion L.	State Supt. of Schools (Ga.)	Articles; confs.
Bruere, Robert W.	Author; social worker	Books on rural sch.; articles; survey of rural church
Burkett, Charles W.	Editor	Books on farming; editor, *American Agriculturist*
Butterfield, K. L.	Ag. educator; rural sociologist	Member, Country Life Comm.; books; articles; confs.
Buttrick, Wallace	Sec'y., Gen. Educ. Board	Articles; supported extension work of Knapp and others

Name	Occupation or Position	Association with Movement
Carney, Mabel	Teacher, normal school	Book on rural sch.; articles; confs.
Carver, Thomas N.	Prof., economics	Articles; books; confs.
Casson, Herbert N.	Editor; free-lance writer	Books; articles
Cattell, James M.	Editor	Articles; editorials on scientific ag. in *Popular Science* and *Scientific American*
Claxton, P. P.	Prof., education	Articles; confs.; promoted rural sch. improvement
Collingwood, H. W.	Editor	Supported sci. ag. in his journal, *Rural New Yorker*
Coulter, John L.	Prof., rural econ.	Book on farmer cooperation; articles; confs.
Crosby, Dick J.	Ag. educator; USDA expert	Bulletins; circulars; confs.
Cubberly, Ellwood P.	Prof., education	Books on rural school; articles
Curtis, Henry S.	Author; lecturer	Book on rural recreation; articles; confs.
Davenport, Eugene	Dean, Coll. of Ag. (Ill.)	Articles on scientific ag.; confs.
Earp, Edwin L.	Sociologist	Book on rural church; surveys
Eastman, Fred	Clergyman	Articles; surveys
Eyerly, Elmer K.	Ag. educator; administrator	Articles on scientific ag.
Fiske, George W.	Dean, Oberlin Grad. Sch. of Theology	Book on country life; articles; confs.
Foght, Harold W.	Ag. educator	Book on rural school; articles; confs.
Galpin, Charles J.	Prof., rural soc.	Book on rural life; articles; confs.
Gates, Frederick T.	Bus. mgr., Rockefeller Foundation	Book on rural school; supported ag. extension work
Gillette, John M.	Rural sociologist	Books on rural sociology; articles, confs.
Glenn, John M.	Dir., Russell Sage Foundation	Supported work investigating rural church conditions; supported Country Life Comm.
Gray Lewis C.	Prof., economics	Articles

Name	Occupation or Position	Association with Movement
Hamilton, John	Farm Institute worker, USDA expert	Articles, confs.
Harger, Charles M.	Editor	Many articles, editorials on country life conditions
Harris, Benjamin F.	Banker	Articles, confs.; chm., Comm. on Ag., Bankers' Assoc.
Hays, Willet M.	Asst. Sec'y. of Ag., USDA expert	Articles; confs.; worked for ag. courses in high schools
Herrick, Myron T.	Lawyer; public servant	Book on rural credits; worked for passage of rural credits legislation
Hibbard, Benjamin H.	Prof., rural econ.	Books; articles on land, tenancy probs., confs.
Hill, James J.	Railroad pres.	Book; articles; confs.; promoted scientific ag.
Holmes, George K.	USDA statistician	Articles; confs.; delegate to Int. Inst. in Rome
Holt, Hamilton	Editor	Editorials in *Independent* supporting all phases of movement
Houston, David F.	Educator, Sec'y. of Agriculture	Articles; gave some support while head of Ag. Dept.
Hurd, William D.	Agricultural educator	Articles; confs.; ag. extension work
Johnson, David B.	Educator, normal school	Articles; confs.; promoted ag. work in normal schools
Kern, Ollie J.	Co. supt. of schools (Ill.)	Book on rural school; articles; boys-girls club work
Knapp, Seaman A.	Ag. educator	Articles; pioneered ag. extension work
Lubin, David	Businessman	Promoted International Institute of Ag., Rome
Lull, Herbert G.	Educator, normal school	Articles on rural school problems
Mann, Albert R.	Agricultural educator	Articles; confs.; promoted scientific ag.
McFarland, J. Horace	Printer	Articles; books on country life; confs.; lectures

Name	Occupation or Position	Association with Movement
McKeever, William A.	Editor; teacher	Book on rural boys and girls; promoted boys-girls work
Monahan, Arthur C.	Education expert, Bur. of Education	Bulletins; articles; surveys; confs.
Morse, Herman N.	Clergyman	Articles; country church work
Myrick, Herbert	Editor; pres., Orange Judd Co.	Articles; book on cooperative finance
Nelson, William L.	Asst. Sec'y of Ag. (Mo.); Congressman	Articles; surveys; confs.
Nourse, Edwin G.	Prof., rural econ.	Articles; confs.
Ousley, Clarence	Editor	Editorial support; served on gov't. comm. studying rural co-ops in Europe, 1913
Page, Walter H.	Editor, publisher, public servant	Member, Country Life Comm.; articles; editorials; worked with Gen. Educ. Bd., Rockefeller Foundation
Pinchot, Gifford	Forester	Member, Country Life Comm.; many activities to promote efficiency in country life
Plunkett, Sir Horace	Irish baron	Articles; book on American rural life; similar activities in Ireland; credited with originating Country Life Comm. idea
Poe, Clarence H.	Editor	Articles; editorials in *Progressive Farmer;* confs.; served on gov't. comm. on ag.
Powell, Edward P.	Journalist	Many articles on country life—many published in *Independent*
Price, Homer C.	Prof., rural economics	Articles; confs.
Quick, J. Herbert	Editor, author	Articles; editorials in *Farm and Fireside;* confs.
Robinson, Leonard G.	Ag. economist; banker	Worked with Jewish ag. groups; articles; confs.

Name	Occupation or Position	Association with Movement
Roosevelt, Theodore	Pres. of U.S.	Appointed Country Life Comm.; articles; addresses
Rosenwald, Julius	Merchant, philanthropist	Gave money to support ag. extension work
Rossiter, William S.	Clerk, Census Bur.; publisher	Articles on rural population matters
Rumely, Edward A.	Manufacturer; educator	Articles; inventions; started Interlaken School
Scudder, Myron T.	Prof., education	Book; articles on rural recreation; confs.
Sears, Jesse B.	Prof., education	Articles on rural education
Shaw, Adele Marie	Journalist	Articles; investigation of rural schools
Shaw, Albert	Editor	Editorial support in *Review of Reviews*
Spillman, William J.	USDA ag. expert	Bulletins; articles; confs.
Sprague, Robert J.	Sociologist	Articles; confs.
Stockbridge, H. E.	Editor	Editorials; articles in *Southern Ruralist;* confs.
Stowe, Lyman B.	Editor	Articles; editorials in *Outlook*
True, Alfred C.	Dir., Off. of Exp. Stations, USDA	Articles; confs.; taught part time in ag. schools
Van Norman, H. E.	Ag. educator	Articles; confs.; worked with farmer associations
Vogt, Paul L.	Prof., Rural Economics and Soc.	Articles; book on rural sociology
Vrooman, Carl B.	Writer; publicist; Asst. Sec'y of Ag.	Articles on scientific farming
Wallace, Henry	Editor	Member, Country Life Comm.; articles; editorials in *Wallaces' Farmer;* confs.
Wiley, Harvey W.	Chemist, USDA	Articles; confs.
Wilson, Warren H.	Clergyman	Work with rural church; articles; books; confs.

Bibliography

Manuscript Collections

Bailey, Liberty Hyde. Papers. Regional History Collection, John M. Olin Research Library. Cornell University. Ithaca, New York.

Baker, Ray Stannard. Papers. Library of Congress. Washington, D.C.

Butterfield, Kenyon Leech. Papers. Library of Congress. Washington, D.C.

Claxton, Philander P. Correspondence of the Commissioner of Education. Bureau of Education, Department of the Interior. Record Group 122. National Archives. Washington, D.C.

Davenport, Eugene. Papers. Archives. University of Illinois. Champaign, Illinois.

Gillette, John M. Papers. Orin G. Libby Manuscript Collection, Chester Fritz Library. University of North Dakota. Grand Forks, North Dakota.

Hibbard, Benjamin H. Papers. Division of Archives, Memorial Library. University of Wisconsin. Madison, Wisconsin.

Houston, David F. Correspondence of the Secretary of Agriculture. Department of Agriculture. Record Group 16. National Archives. Washington, D.C.

James, Edmund J. Papers. Archives. University of Illinois. Champaign, Illinois.

Pinchot, Gifford. Papers. Library of Congress. Washington, D.C.

Roosevelt, Theodore. Papers. Library of Congress. Washington, D.C.

Wallace, Henry. Papers. Special Collections, University Library. University of Iowa. Iowa City, Iowa.

Wiley, Harvey W. Papers. Library of Congress. Washington, D.C.

State and Federal Publications

Cornell University. Agricultural Experiment Station. *An Agricultural Survey of Ithaca, Dryden, Danby, and Lansing Townships, Tompkins County, New York,* by George F. Warren and K. C. Livermore. Bulletin No. 295. Ithaca, New York.

————. *Cornell Nature Study Leaflet,* No. 3. Ithaca, New York. March, 1904.

North Carolina. *North Carolina High School Bulletin,* V. Chapel Hill, July, 1914.

United States. *Statistical Abstract of the United States, 1910, 1920, 1930.* Washington: Government Printing Office, 1911, 1921, 1931.

————. *Statutes at Large,* Vol. XXIX, Part 2, "Income Tax," 756–57, 761–62 (December, 1915–March, 1917).

U. S. Bureau of Education. *Reports of the Commissioner of Education,* 1909–1920. Washington: Government Printing Office, 1909–1920.

U. S. Bureau of the Census. *Thirteenth Census of the United States, 1910.* Washington: Government Printing Office, 1911.

U. S. Congress. *Congressional Record,* 60th Cong., 2d sess., 1909, XLIII, Part 3, 3118–20, 3310; Part 4, 3660–64.

————. *Report of the Country Life Commission.* Senate Doc. 705, 60th Cong., 2d sess., 1909.

————. *Report of the Public Lands Commission.* Senate Doc. 183, 55th Cong., 3d sess., 1905.

U. S. Department of Agriculture. *Farmers' Institutes and Agricultural Extension Work in the United States in 1913,* by John Hamilton. Bulletin No. 83. Washington: Government Printing Office, 1914.

————. *Farmers' Institutes for Women,* by John Hamilton, Circular No. 85. Washington: Government Printing Office, 1909.

————. *A History of Agricultural Education in the United States, 1785–1925,* by Alfred C. True. Miscellaneous Publication No. 36. Washington: Government Printing Office, 1929.

————. *A History of Extension Work in the United States, 1785–1923,* by Alfred C. True. Miscellaneous Publication No. 15. Washington: Government Printing Office, 1928.

————. Office of the Secretary. *Social and Labor Needs of Farm Women,* Report No. 103; *Domestic Needs of Farm Women,* Report No. 104; *Educational Needs of Farm Women,* Report No. 105; *Economic Needs of Farm Women,* Report No. 106. Washington: Government Printing Office, 1915.

————. *Yearbooks, 1901–1919, 1940.* Washington: Government Printing Office, 1902–1920, 1940.

Proceedings and Reports of Organizations

Association of American Agricultural Colleges and Experiment Stations. *Proceedings of Annual Convention, 1904–1920.*

First Wisconsin Country Life Conference. Bulletin of the University of Wisconsin, Serial 472, Series 308. February, 1911.

Illinois Bankers' Association. *Proceedings of the Twenty–Second Annual Convention, 1912.*

Illinois Federation for Country Life Progress. *Third Annual Convention, 1913.*

Iowa Bankers' Association. *Proceedings of the Twenty–Sixth Annual Convention, 1912.*

National Conference of Social Work, *Proceedings, 1908.*

National Country Life Association. *Proceedings of the First National Country Life Conference, 1919.*

National Education Association. *Proceedings and Addresses, 1897, 1900–1919.*

Pennsylvania Rural Progress Association. *Report of the President and Secretary.* December 20, 1912.

"Report of the Committee of Twelve on Rural Schools." National Education Association. *Proceedings and Addresses, 1897,* 385–583.

Western New York Horticultural Society. *Proceedings of Fifty–Sixth Annual Meeting, 1911.* Rochester, New York.

Unpublished Dissertations

Clutts, Betty Carol. "Country Life Aspects of the Progressive Movement." Unpublished Ph.D. Dissertation, Ohio State University, 1962.

Keppel, Anna Marie. "Country Schools for Country Children: Backgrounds of the Reform Movement in Rural Elementary Education, 1890–1914." Unpublished Ph.D. Dissertation, University of Wisconsin, 1960.

Tweton, Donald Jerome. "The Attitudes and Policies of the Theodore Roosevelt Administration Toward American Agriculture." Unpublished Ph.D. Dissertation, University of Oklahoma, 1964.

Articles

"Agriculture the True Source of Our Wealth." *Scientific American,* XCV (September 29, 1906), 226.

"Appreciations of Sir Horace Plunkett." *Rural America,* X (May, 1932), 7.

Aronovici, Carol. "Liberty Hyde Bailey." *Survey,* LXXXVII (March, 1951), 122–27.

Bailey, Liberty Hyde. "An Appeal to the Teachers of New York State." *Cornell Nature–Study Leaflet,* No. 3 (March, 1904), Cornell University, Ithaca, New York, pp. 1–11.

————. "The Collapse of Freak Farming." *Country Life in America,* IV (May, 1903), 14–16.

————. "The Common Schools and the Farm Youth." *Century,* LXXIV (October, 1907), 960–67.

————. "Country Living in the Next Generation." *Independent,* LXXXV (March 6, 1916), 336–38.

————. "An Evolutionists's View of Nature and Religion." *Independent,* LI (February 2, 1899), 335–39.

————. "Moon Farming." *Independent,* LXVII (October 14, 1909), 907–09.

————. "The New Education." *Country Life in America,* V (November, 1903), 34–35.

————. "The Place of Agriculture in Higher Education." *Education,* XXXI (December, 1910), 249–56.

————. "Rural Development in Relation to Social Welfare." National Conference of Social Work. *Proceedings, 1908,* pp. 83–91.

————. "School Gardens: The New Movement in the School That Improves the Grounds and Provides a Laboratory Out-of-Doors." *Country Life in America,* III (March, 1903), 190–92.

————. "Some Aspects of the Country–Life Movement." *North Carolina High School Bulletin,* V (July, 1914), 96–105.

————. "A State Program for Rural Betterment." Western New York Horticultural Society, *Proceedings of Fifty–Sixth Annual Meeting, 1911,* Rochester, New York, 40–43.

————. "What This Magazine Stands For." *Country Life in America,* I (November, 1901), 24–25.

————. "Why Do the Boys Leave the Farm?" *Century,* LXXII (July, 1906), 410–16.

————. "Why Do Some Boys Take to Farming?" *Century,* LXXII (August, 1906), 612–17.

————. "Wise Words on Rural Credits." *Banker–Farmer,* I (January, 1914), 6.

"Banker–Farmer Alliance for Cooperation." *Survey,* XXXII (July 24, 1915), 383.

"Bankers and Farmers." *Outlook,* CI (August 31, 1912), 997–98.

Baruch, Bernard. "Some Aspects of the Farmers' Problems." *Atlantic Monthly,* CXXVIII (July, 1921), 111–20.

Bell, John E. "From the Man Who Holds the Plow." *Outlook,* XCI (April 10, 1909), 826–29.

Bill, Arthur J. "What's the Matter With the Farmer? Another View of the Commission's Report." *Farm and Fireside,* XXXIII (June, 10, 1909).

"Birth–Control and Race–Suicide." *Literary Digest,* LIV (February 3, 1917), 244–45.

Bisland, Elizabeth. "Societies for Minding One's Own Business." *North American Review,* CXCII (November, 1910), 623–29.

Boisen, Anton T. "Factors Which Have to Do With the Decline of the Country Church." *American Journal of Sociology,* XXII (September, 1916), 177–92.

Bramhall, J. T. "Back to the Soil Movement in California." *Survey,* XXXI (January 24, 1914), 486–87.

"Bringing City and Farm Women Together." *Survey,* XXXV (February 19, 1916), 616.

Butterfield, Kenyon L. "Can Rural Social Forces Be Federated?—A First Step." *Review of Reviews,* XXV (April, 1902), 455–57.

——. "The Training of Rural Leaders." *Survey,* XXXII (October 3, 1914), 13–14.

Buttrick, Wallace. "The Beginning and Aims of the General Education Board." *National Education Association, Proceedings and Addresses, 1903,* pp. 116–23.

Callicotte, William R. "Discussion." *National Education Association, Proceedings and Addresses, 1909,* pp. 971–72.

Carter, Thomas H. "Postal Savings Banks." *Independent,* LXVI (January 14, 1909), 73–77.

Carver, Thomas N. "Economic Significance of Changes in Country Population." *Annals of the American Academy of Political and Social Science,* XL (March, 1912), 21–25.

——. "Life in the Corn Belt." *World's Work,* VII (December, 1903), 4232–39.

——. "The Work of Rural Organization." *Journal of Political Economy,* XXII (November, 1914), 821–44.

Casson, Herbert N. "The New American Farmer." *Review of Reviews,* XXXVII (May, 1908), 598–602.

"Cheaper Money for the Farmer." *Literary Digest,* LIII (July 29, 1916), 236–37.

"The Church and Rural Progress." *Survey,* XXXI (October 25, 1913), 96.

"The Cities and the Farm Movement." *World's Work,* XXVI (May, 1913), 27–28.

Collins, Paul V. "Will the Rural Credits Law Work?" *Outlook,* CXIII (August 2, 1916), 780, 789–92.

"The Commission on Country Life." *World's Work,* XVII, (November, 1908), 10860–61.

"Community Engineer vs. Community Leader." *Survey,* XXX (August 30, 1913), 656–57.

Comstock, Anna Botsford. "Nature–Study and Agriculture." *Nature–Study Review,* (July, 1905), p. 147.

"A Conference on Rural Life." *Outlook,* XCVI (September 3, 1910), 8–9.

Cook, Ellen. "Letter From a Farmer's Wife." *American Magazine,* LXVII (April, 1909), 630.

"The Consolidation of Rural Schools," *American City,* IX (December, 1913), 577–79.

"The Country Church." *Nation,* LXXXVIII (June 17, 1909), 599.

"Country Improvements." *Independent,* LIV (April 17, 1902), 946–48.

"The Country Life Commission." *Springfield Republican* (Springfield, Massachusetts), November 7, 1908.

"The Country Life Commission and the Church." *Independent,* LXVII (August 26, 1909), 489–91.

"The Country Life Commission, How Much Did It Accomplish?" *Country Gentleman,* LXXIV (March 11, 1909), 231.

"Country Life Problems." *Nation,* LXXXIX (November 18, 1909), 479–80.

"The Country School." *Independent.* LXIX (October 13, 1910), 882–84.

"The Country vs. the City." *Wallaces' Farmer,* XXXIV (January 8, 1909), 43.

Cox, Lawanda F. "Tenancy in the United States, 1865–1900: A Consideration of the Validity of the Agricultural Ladder Hypothesis." *Agricultural History,* XVIII (July, 1944), 97–105.

"Credit for Farmers." *World's Work,* XXVII (January, 1914), 252–53.

Crosby, Dick J. "How May the Rural Schools Be More Closely Related to the Life and Needs of the People?" National Education Association, *Proceedings and Addresses, 1909,* 969–71.

Curtis, Wardon A. "What Is the Matter With Farming?" *Independent,* LXVII (December 30, 1909), 1484–88.

Davenport, Eugene. "Scientific Farming." *Annals of the American Academy of Political and Social Science,* XL (March, 1912), 45–50.

Davis, Rodney O. "Iowa Farm Opinion and the Good Roads Movement, 1903–1904." *Annals of Iowa,* 3rd Series, XXXVII (Summer, 1964), 321–38.

Deiman, Henry. "The Institutional Church for the Rural Community." *Survey,* XXX (May 24, 1913), 280–82.

Dewey, John. "The School as a Social Center." National Education Association, *Proceedings and Addresses, 1902,* 373–83.

Dille, Alvin. "The Reorganization of the Country School." United States Department of Agriculture, *Yearbook, 1919* (Washington: Government Printing Office, 1920), 289–306.

"Doctor of Agriculture—A New Profession." *World's Work,* XXIV (September, 1912), 499–500.

Eastman, Fred. "Rural Churches That Do Their Job." *World's Work,* XXV (March, 1913), 585–88.

Editoral comment on Country Life Commission. *Sacramento Union,* November 30, 1908, p. 6; *San Francisco Chronicle,* November 19, 1908.

"Editor's Diary." *North American Review,* CLXXXIII (September 21, 1906), 567–69.

Ellsworth, Clayton S. "The Coming of Rural Consolidated Schools to the Ohio Valley, 1892–1912." *Agricultural History,* XXX (July, 1956), 119–28.

————. "Theodore Roosevelt's Country Life Commission." *Agricultural History,* XXXIV (October, 1960), 155–72.

"Equipment of Some Michigan Country Schools." *Survey,* XXXI (January 10, 1914), 445.

Everitt, James A. "The New Farmers' Movement." *Independent,* LXII May 23, 1907), 1197–99.

"The Exodus of Farmers." *Wallaces' Farmer*, XXXIII (September 25, 1908), 1146.

"Expansion by Irrigation." *World's Work*, IV (August, 1902), 2365.

Eyerly, E. K. "Co-operative Movements Among Farmers." *Annals of the American Academy of Political and Social Science*, XL (March, 1912), 58–68.

"Farm and City." *New York Times*, November 27, 1913, p. 12.

"The Farm Commission." *Independent*, LXV (October 29, 1908), 1012–14.

"Farm Immigrants." *Independent*, LXXIII (September 12, 1912), 631.

"The Farm Labor Problem." *Wallaces' Farmer*, XXXVI (February 10, 1911), 214.

"The Farm Life Commission." *Wallaces' Farmer*, XXXIII (August 21, 1908), 994.

"Farm Papers on Rural Uplift." *Literary Digest*, XXXVII (December 26, 1908), 965–66.

"Farm Wives Tell of Further Needs." *New York Times*, April 4, 1915, Part IV, p. 6.

"Farm Women Find Life Hard." *New York Times*, May 30, 1915, Part V, pp. 14–15.

"Farmer Colonies for Land Hungry." *New York Times*, June 20, 1915, Part II, p. 6.

"The Farmers and the Future." *World's Work*, XV (February, 1908), 9846–48.

"Farmers and Others." *New Republic*, XVI (September 7, 1918), 155–56.

"The Farmer's Problems." *Independent*, LXIII (September 12, 1907), 645–46.

A Farmer's Wife. "The Child and the Farm." *Outlook*, XCI (April 10, 1909), 832–33.

"Farms Neglected, Houston's Warning." *New York Times*, November 15, 1913, p. 10.

Foght, Harold W. "The Country School." *Annals of the American Academy of Political and Social Science*, XL (March, 1912), 149–57.

"For Good Roads." *Outlook*, XCV (August 27, 1910), 918.

"For a More Satisfactory Country Life." *Wallaces' Farmer*, XXXIV (October 22, 1909), 1338.

Fuller, Wayne E. "The Rural Roots of the Progressive Leaders." *Agricultural History*, XLII (January, 1968), 1–13.

Galpin, Charles. "The Development of the Science and Philosophy of American Rural Society." *Agricultural History*, XII (July, 1938), 195–208.

Gee, Wilson. "A Qualitative Study of Rural Depopulation in a Single Township, 1900–1930." *American Journal of Sociology*, XXXIX (September, 1933), 210–21.

————, and Dewees Runk. "Qualitative Selections in Cityward Migration." *American Journal of Sociology,* XXXVII (September, 1931), 254–65.

Gillette, John M. "City Trend of Population and Leadership." *Quarterly Journal of the University of North Dakota,* I (October 1910), 54–76; (January, 1911), 117–24.

"The Great Country Life Movement." *World's Work,* XXIII (April 12, 1912), 615–19.

Greathouse, Charles A. "Free Delivery of Rural Mails." United States Department of Agriculture, *Yearbook, 1900* (Washington: Government Printing Office, 1901), 513–28.

Gregory, Clifford V. "Farming by Special Train." *Outlook,* XCVII (August 22, 1911) 913–22.

Grupe, Mary A. "How the Problems of the Rural Schools Are Being Met." *Popular Science,* LXXXIII (November, 1913), 484–90.

Haggard, H. Rider. "Back to the Land." *World Today,* XL (December, 1906), 1261–64.

Hall, C. N. "Our Country Towns." *New England Magazine,* n.s. XXII (September, 1900), 50–55.

Halstead, William. "The Automatic Farm." *Outlook,* XCI (July 31, 1909), 812–13.

"Hardware Section." *Iron Age,* LXXXII (October 1, 1908), 960.

Harger, Charles M. "The Country Banker's Awakening; How the Bank May Cooperate With the Farm for Their Mutual Advantage." *Independent,* LXXV (September 11, 1913), 611–15.

Harris, B. F. "What I Am Trying to Do." *World's Work,* XXVI (August, 1913), 433–34.

Hays, Charles Lepley. "Relations of Farmer and Factory Worker." *Cyclopedia of American Agriculture.* Edited by L. H. Bailey. New York: The Macmillan Company 1909, IV, 198–200.

Hibbard, Benjamin Horace, "Compensating Tenants for Improvements." Typescript in Hibbard MSS. University of Wisconsin. Madison.

————. "Farm Tenancy in the United States." *Annals of the American Academy of Political and Social Science,* XL (March, 1912), 29–39.

Hill, Edna M. "The Little Red Schoolhouse a 'Fake'; What the Country Schoolhouse Really Is and Why." *Independent,* LXXV (August 7, 1913), 316–18.

Hoagland, H. E. "The Movement of Rural Population in Illinois." *Journal of Political Economy,* XX (November, 1912), 913–27.

"Hobbling Back to Nature." *Nation,* LXXIV (March 21, 1907) 259–60.

Holmes, G. K. "Movement From City and Town to Farms." United States Department of Agriculture, *Yearbook, 1914* (Washington: Government Printing Office, 1915), 257–74.

Holmes, Roy Hinman. "The Passing of the Farmer." *Atlantic Monthly,* CX (October, 1912), 517–23.

Hutchinson, Woods. "Overworked Children on the Farm and in the School." *Annals of the American Academy of Political and*

Social Science, XXXIII (Supplement, March, 1909) 116–21.

"Indiana 'Putting It Up' to the Public." *Survey,* XXXI (December 13, 1913), 309.

"Interest of Bankers in Agricultural Education." *New York Times,* May 6, 1913, p. 12.

"An Interstate Agricultural Congress." *World's Work,* XXVII (July, 1914), 256.

"It Must Come." *Independent,* LXVII (October 28, 1909), 986–87.

"James J. Hill's Advice." *Independent* LXXIII (September 12, 1912), 632–33.

Johnstone, Paul L. "Old Ideals Versus New Ideas in Farm Life." *Farmers in a Changing World,* United States Department of Agriculture, Yearbook, 1940 (Washington: Government Printing Office, 1941), pp. 111–70.

Kates, Clarence S. "Origin and Growth of Rural Conferences." *Annals of the American Academy of Political and Social Science,* XL (March, 1912), 110–16.

Kemp, Norval. "Statement on Work, Purposes, Etc. of the Country Life Commission." Typescript in Bailey MSS. Cornell University, Ithaca.

Kern, O. J. "The Consolidated School and the New Agriculture." National Education Association, *Proceedings and Addresses, 1907,* pp. 277–79.

Kinley, David. "The Movement of Population from Country to City." *Cyclopedia of American Agriculture.* Edited by L. H. Bailey. New York: The Macmillan Company, 1909, IV, 113–19.

Knapp, H. E. "Director Bailey from the Standpoint of a Farmer." *Cornell Countryman,* XI (December, 1913), 94.

Knapp, Seaman A. "Agricultural Education for the Rural Districts." National Education Association, *Proceedings and Addresses, 1909,* 954–59.

———. "An Agricultural Revolution." *World's Work,* XII (July, 1906) 7733–38.

———. "The Farmers' Cooperative Demonstration Work." United States Department of Agriculture, *Yearbook, 1909* (Washington: Government Printing Office, 1910), 153–60.

Larson, Olaf F. "Liberty Hyde Bailey's Impact on Rural Life." *Baileya,* VI (March, 1958), 10-21.

Lawrence, George H. M. "Liberty Hyde Bailey, 1858–1954." *Baileya,* III (March, 1955), 27–40.

"Liberty Hyde Bailey, Botanist, Dead." *New York Times,* December 27, 1954, p. 17.

"The Louisville Convention for Rural Betterment." *Outlook,* CVII (May 9, 1914), 57.

Lyle, Eugene P., Jr. "A Corn Gospel Train." *World's Work,* XII (May, 1906), 7515–20.

Main, J. H. T. "Western Land Problems: The Rapid Rise in the Price of Land Produces a Critical Situation." *Independent,* LXXIV (January 30, 1913), 250–52.

Malin, James C. "The Background of the First Bills to Establish a Bureau of Markets, 1911–1912." *Agricultural History,* VI (July, 1932), 107–29.

"The Malthusian Theory in the Light of Recent Statistics." *Review of Reviews,* VI (December, 1892), 588–600.

Mann, A. R. "Life of Liberty Hyde Bailey." *Cornell Countryman,* XI (December, 1913), 69–73.

Marshall, Edward. "Bankers Find Profit in Making Better Farmers." *New York Times,* May 11, 1913, Part V, p. 6.

Meyer, George Von Lengerke. "Postal Savings Banks." *Independent,* LXIV (January 2, 1908), 9–11.

"Milk and Water." *Country Gentleman,* LXXIV (February 18, 1909), 156.

Miller, E. E. "Why Farmers Must Work Together." *Southern Agriculturalist,* XLV (January 1, 1915), 7.

Mitchell, Edward B. "The American Farm Woman as She Sees Herself." United States Department of Agriculture, *Yearbook, 1914* (Washington: Government Printing Office, 1915), 311–18.

Monahan, Arthur C. "Development of Rural Schools a Problem of Tremendous Importance, Says Government Expert." *New York Times,* April 13, 1913, Part VII, p. 11.

————. "Rural Education." *Report of the Commissioner of Education, 1913* (Washington: Government Printing Office, 1914), I, 157–210.

"More Money for the Farmer." *Independent,* LXXV (August 14, 1913), 367–68.

Morse, Herman N. "Marketing and Farm Credits." *Survey,* XXX (May 10, 1913), 214–15.

Mosse, George L. "The Mystical Origins of National Socialism." *Journal of the History of Ideas,* XXII (January–March, 1961), 81–96.

"National Conference on Rural Education and Rural Life." *School and Society,* V (March 31, 1917), 389–90.

"National Conference on Rural Education at the University of Pennsylvania." *School and Society,* V (April 28, 1917), 508–10.

Nelson, W. L. "The Farmers on Farm Life; The Opinions of the Men on the Land in Missouri." *World's Work,* XXIII(November, 1911), 77–79.

"New England Conference to Promote Rural Progress." *Survey,* XXX (April 12, 1913), 55–56.

"New Era for Farm Women." *Good Housekeeping,* XLIV (July, 1909), 39–45.

"Now the President Plans to Aid the Farmer." *New York Times,* May 24, 1908, Part V, p. 9.

"Our Farmers Move Often." *New York Times,* May 20, 1914, p. 12.

"Our Washington Letter." *Country Gentleman,* LXXIII (November 26, 1908), 1128.

Ousley, Clarence. "The Beginnings of Rural Credit." *Outlook,* CXII

(June 28, 1916). 511–15.

Page, Walter Hines. "The Hookworm and Civilization." *World's Work,* XXIV (September, 1912), 504–18.

――――――. "The Man Who Owns the Land." *World's Work,* XX (August, 1910), 10860.

"Parcels Post." *Wallaces' Farmer,* XXXIV (November 12, 1909) 1450.

Parker, Harold. "Good Roads Movement." *Annals of the American Academy of Political and Social Science,* XL (March, 1912), 51–57.

Parsons, E. R. "Henry Wallace's Estimate of Dry Land Farming." *Western Farm Life,* XVII (December 1, 1915), 5–8.

"Paternalism." *Country Gentleman,* LXXIII (November 12, 1908), 1084.

Pearse, R. A. "How to Keep the Young Folks on the Farms." *Farm Journal,* XXXII (October, 1908), 374.

Pearson, Mrs. Edward N. "City Rest Rooms." *American City,* III (July, 1910), 27–28.

Peer, F. S. "What Is the Matter With Agriculture?" *Country Gentleman,* LXXIII (December 17, 1908), 1197–98.

Phelps, Arthur S. "The Coming Exodus." *Arena,* XXXV (April, 1906), 390–91.

"Plans for Rural Utopia." *New York Times,* June 1, 1915, p. 18.

Plunkett, Sir Horace. "Conservation and Rural Life; An Irish View of Two Roosevelt Policies." *Outlook,* XCIV (January 29, 1910), 260–64.

――――――. "The Neglected Farmer." *Outlook,* XCIV (February 5, 1910), 298–302.

"The Plutocratic Farmer." *Wallaces' Farmer,* XXXIII (November 27, 1908), 1450.

Poe, Clarence H. "Farmer Children Need Farmer Studies." *World's Work,* VI (August, 1903), 3760–62.

"Postal Savings." *Survey,* XXIII (October 16, 1909), 85–86.

"Prefer to Uplift Themselves." *New York Times,* November 19, 1908, p. 8.

"Presidential Anxiety for the Farmer." *Literary Digest,* XXVII (August 22, 1908), 235–36.

"The President's Concern." *Farm Journal,* XXXII (October, 1908), 380.

"Problems of the Country Church." *Literary Digest,* LII (May 6, 1916), 1282.

"The Railroad Missionary." *New York Times,* October 15, 1913, p. 14.

"A Remarkable Study of a Rural Community." *World's Work,* XXVI (July, 1913), 263–64.

Roberts, Albert E., and Henry Israel. "Rural Work of the Young Men's Christian Association." *Annals of the American Academy of Political and Social Science,* XL (March, 1912), 140–48.

Roberts, Isaac P. "The Farmer and His Profits." *Outlook,* XCII (May

8, 1909), 91–92.

Roosevelt, Theodore. "Rural Life." *Outlook,* XCV (August 27, 1910), 919–22.

_____. "The Welfare of the Farmers." *Outlook,* C (April 20, 1912), 852–56.

Ross, Earle D. "Roosevelt and Agriculture." *Mississippi Valley Historical Review,* XIV (December, 1927), 287–310.

Ross, Edward Alsworth. "Folk Depletion as a Cause of Rural Decline." *Publications of the American Sociological Society,* XI (1916), 21–30.

Ross, Joseph B. "The Agrarian Revolution in the Middle West." *North American Review,* CXC (September, 1909), 376–91.

Rossiter, William S. "The Decrease in Rural Population." *Review of Reviews,* XXIV (July, 1906), 74–80.

_____. "The Pressure of Population." *Atlantic Monthly,* CXVIII (December, 1911), 836–43.

Rumely, Edward A. "The Passing of the Man With the Hoe." *World's Work,* XX (August, 1910), 13246–58.

"Rural Leaders on Their Problems." *Survey* XXX (August 30, 1913), 655–56.

"Rural Life and Education." *Independent,* LII (July 5, 1900), 1631–32.

"Rural Life Conference Held at the University of Virginia." United States Bureau of Education, *Report of the Commissioner of Education, 1909* (Washington: Government Printing Office, 1910), I, 83–84.

"Rural Uplift in the Southwest." *Literary Digest,* XXXIX (May 22, 1909), 874.

"A St. Lawrence County Farmer." *Post–Standard* (Syracuse, New York), October 22, 1908.

Sanderson Dwight. "Country–Life Forces Mobilizing." *Review of Reviews,* LXIII (April, 1921), 421–25.

"School for Rural Social Workers." *Survey,* XXX (July 26, 1913), 556.

Scudder, Myron T. "Rural Recreation, A Socializing Factor." *Annals of the American Academy of Political and Social Science,* XL (March, 1912), 175–90.

Sears, J. B. "The Problem for the Rural School." *Popular Science,* LXXXVI (February, 1915), 174–79.

Shelby, Mary Doane. "An Open Letter to Secretary Houston From a Farmer's Wife." *Outlook,* CXI (December 15, 1915), 923–25.

Sherwood, Herbert Francis. "Taking Thought for American Agriculture." *Outlook,* LCV (August 13, 1910), 843–45.

"The Social Problems of the Farmer." *American Journal of Sociology,* VIII (September, 1902), 281–83.

"Some Solid Reasons for a Strike of Farm Wives." *Literary Digest,* LXIII (December 20, 1919), 74, 78.

Spillman, William J. "The Agricultural Ladder." *American Economic*

Review, IX (Supplement, March, 1919), 170–79.

————. "Efficiency Movement in Its Relation to Agriculture." *Annals of the American Academy of Political and Social Science,* LIX (May, 1915), 65–76.

Stowe, Lyman Beecher. "Training City Boys for Country Life." *Outlook,* CII (November 9, 1912), 537–41; (November 16, 1912), 584–91.

"Taffy for the Farmer." *Wallaces' Farmer,* XXXIII (September 4, 1908) 1050.

Taylor, Graham Romeyn. "From Plowed Land to Pavement; The Government's Hand in Helping the City Dweller by Helping the Farmer." *Survey,* XXXVI (April 1, 1916), 20–26.

"Teaching the Farmer to Play." *Nation,* XCIV (March 28, 1912), 307–08.

"Teaching the Teachers." *Wallaces' Farmer,* XXXIV (October 15, 1909), 792.

"Theology and Country Life." *Independent,* LXXVII, May 11, 1914), 237–38.

Trimble, William J. "The Influence of the Passing of the Public Lands." *Atlantic Monthly,* CXIII (June, 1914), 754–58.

True, Alfred C. "Some Problems of the Rural Common School." United States Department of Agriculture, *Yearbook, 1901* (Washington: Government Printing Office, 1902), 133–54.

Vance, Truman S. "Why Young Men Leave the Farms." *Independent,* LXX (March 16, 1911), 553–60.

Van Cortland, R. B. "What Is Agricultural Credit?" *North American Review,* CXCIX (April, 1914), 585–88.

Vontrees, Ross. "A Farmer Speaks." *New Republic,* XXI (February 4, 1920), 291–93.

Vrooman, Carl. "Cooperation a Great Hope," *New York Times,* December 19, 1915, Part VIII, p. 8.

————. "The Agricultural Revolution." *Century,* XCIII (November, 1916), 111–23.

Vrooman, Frank. "Uncle Sam's Romance With Science and the Soil." *Arena,* XXXV (January, 1906), 36–46.

Wallace, Henry. "The Socialization of Farm Life." Typescript of article prepared for *Youth's Companion* magazine in Wallace MSS. University of Iowa. Iowa City.

"Waste Land." *Independent,* LXIX (July 21, 1910), 153–54.

Weeks, Arland D. "The Question of Agricultural Population." *Popular Science,* LXXXIV (March, 1914), 251–56.

Welliver, Judson C. "Eliminating the Middleman Between Farmer and Consumer." *Munsey's Magazine,* XLIX (April, 1913), 63–70.

Wells, George F. "The Country Church." *Cyclopedia of American Agriculture.* Edited by L. H. Bailey. New York: The Macmillan Company, 1909, IV, 297–303.

————. "The Country Church and Its Social Problem." *Outlook,*

LXXXIII (August 18, 1906), 893–95.

————. "Is An Organized Country Life Movement Possible?" *Survey,* XXIX (January 4, 1913), 449–56.

————. "The Rural Church." *Annals of the American Academy of Political and Social Science,* XL (March, 1912), 131–39.

"What Do the Farmers Want?" *New York Evening Journal,* August 11, 1908.

"What Really Troubles Cornell." *Chicago Evening Post,* October 2, 1911.

"What the Country School Must Be." *World's Work,* XVII (April, 1909), 11417–18.

"Why Young Women Are Leaving Our Farms." *Literary Digest,* LXVII (October 2, 1920), 56–58.

Wiley, Harvey W. "Rural Sanitation." Typescript, dated 1910 in Wiley MSS. Library of Congress.

"Will Farmers Help Themselves?" *Independent,* LXVI (March 18, 1909), 594–95.

Wilson, Owen. "Railroading Knowledge to the Farmers." *World's Work,* XXIII (November, 1911), 100–06.

Wilson, Warren H. "The Church and the Rural Community." *American Journal of Sociology,* XVI (March, 1911), 668–93.

————. "Farm Cooperation for Better Business, Schools, and Churches," *Survey,* XXXVI (April 8, 1916), 51–53.

————. "Social Life in the Country." *Annals of the American Academy of Political and Social Science,* XL (March, 1912), 119–30.

Wooley, Mary E. "The Woman's Club Woman." *Good Housekeeping,* L (May, 1910), 559–62.

Wright, Edward A. "The Hill Town Problem." *New England Magazine,* n.s. XXIV (August, 1901), 622–26.

"The Wrong Remedy." *Country Gentleman,* LXXIII (August 20, 1908), 790.

Zimmerman, Carle C. "The Migration to Towns and Cities." *American Journal of Sociology,* XXXII (November, 1926), 450–55; XXXIII (July, 1927), 105–09; XXXIII (September, 1927), 237–41.

————, and Lynn Smith. "Migration to Towns and Cities." *American Journal of Sociology,* XXXVI (July, 1930), 41–51.

Books, Monographs, and Pamphlets

Agresti, Olivia Rossetti. *David Lubin: A Study in Practical Idealism.* 2nd Edition. Berkeley and Los Angeles: University of California Press, 1941.

Atkeson, Thomas C. *Semi–Centennial History of the Patrons of Husbandry.* New York: Orange Judd Company, 1916.

Bailey, Joseph Cannon. *Seaman A. Knapp: Schoolmaster of American Agriculture.* New York: The Macmillan Company, 1945.

Bailey, Liberty Hyde. *The Country Life Movement in the United*

States. New York: The Macmillan Company, 1911.

_____(ed). *Cyclopedia of American Agriculture: A Popular Survey of Agricultural Conditions, Practices and Ideals in the United States and Canada.* 4 volumes. New York: The Macmillan Company, 1907–1909.

_____. *Ground–Levels in Democracy.* Published privately. Ithaca, New York, 1916.

_____. *The Harvest of the Year to the Tiller of the Soil.* New York: The Macmillan Company, 1927.

_____. *The Holy Earth.* New York: Charles Scribner's Sons, 1915.

_____. *The Nature–Study Idea: An Interpretation of the New School–Movement to Put the Young Into Relation and Sympathy with Nature.* 3rd Edition. New York: The Macmillan Company, 1909.

_____. *The Outlook to Nature.* New and Revised Edition. New York: The Macmillan Company, 1911.

_____. *The Seven Stars.* New York: The Macmillan Company, 1923.

_____. *The State and the Farmer.* New York: The Macmillan Company, 1908.

_____. *The Training of Farmers.* New York: The Century Company, 1910.

_____. *Universal Service, the Hope of Humanity.* New York: Sturgis and Walton Company, 1918.

_____. *What Is Democracy?* Published privately. Ithaca, New York.

_____. *York State Rural Problems.* 2 volumes. Albany, New York: J. B. Lyon Company, 1913, 1915.

Barrett, Charles. *The Mission, History and Times of the Farmers' Union.* Nashville: Marshall and Bruce Company, 1909.

Benedict, Murray R. *Farm Policies of the United States, 1790–1950: A Study of Their Origins and Development.* New York: Twentieth Century Fund, 1953.

Betts, George Herbert. *New Ideals in Rural Schools.* Boston: Houghton Mifflin Company, 1913.

Bricker, Garland A. *Solving the Country Church Problem.* Cincinnati: Jennings and Graham, 1913.

Brunner, Edmund deSchweinitz. *The Growth of a Science: A Half–Century of Rural Sociological Research in the United States.* New York: Harper and Brothers, 1957.

Buck, Solon Justus. *The Granger Movement: A Study of Agricultural Organization and Its Political, Economic, and Social Manifestations, 1870–1880.* Cambridge: Harvard University Press, 1913.

Burritt, M. C. *The County Agent and the Farm Bureau.* New York: Harcourt and Brace, 1922.

Butterfield, Kenyon L. *Chapters in Rural Progress.* Chicago: University of Chicago Press, 1908.

_____. *The Country Church and the Rural Problem.* Chicago: University of Chicago Press, 1911.

Carney, Mabel. *Country Life and the Country School: A Study of the Agencies of Rural Progress and of the Social Relationship of the School and the Community.* Chicago: Row, Peterson and Company, 1912.

Cline, Rodney. *The Life and Work of Seaman A. Knapp.* Contributions to Education No. 183. Nashville: George Peabody College for Teachers, 1936.

Collins, T. Byard. *The New Agriculture: A Popular Outline of the Changes Which Are Revolutionizing the Methods of Farming and the Habits of Farm Life.* New York: Munn and Company, 1906.

Cowles, Anna Roosevelt. *Letters From Theodore Roosevelt to Anna Roosevelt Cowles, 1870–1914.* New York: Charles Scribner's Sons, 1924.

Cremin, Lawrence A. *The Transformation of the School: Progressivism in American Education, 1876–1957.* New York: Alfred A. Knopf, 1961.

Croly, Herbert. *The Promise of American Life.* New York: The Macmillan Company, 1909.

Cubberly, Ellwood P. *Changing Conceptions of Education.* Boston: Houghton Mifflin Company, 1909.

————. *The Improvement of Rural Schools.* Boston: Houghton Mifflin Company, 1912.

————. *Rural Life and Education; A Study of the Rural–School Problem As a Phase of the Rural–Life Problem.* Boston: Houghton Mifflin Company, 1914.

Cutright, Paul. *Theodore Roosevelt, The Naturalist.* New York: Harper and Brothers, 1956.

Davenport, Eugene. *Education for Efficiency.* Boston: D. C. Heath and Company, 1909.

Dewey, John. *My Pedagogic Creed.* New York: E. L. Kellogg and Company, 1897.

————. *The School and Society:* Revised Edition. Chicago: University of Chicago Press, 1900, 1915.

Digby, Margaret. *Sir Horace Plunkett: An Anglo–American Irishman.* Oxford: Basil Blackwell, 1949.

Dorf, Philip. *Liberty Hyde Bailey: An Informal Biography.* Ithaca: Cornell University Press, 1956.

Earp, Edwin L. *The Social Engineer.* New York: Eaton and Mains, 1911.

Emmet, Boris, and John E. Jeuck. *Catalogues and Counters: A History of Sears, Roebuck and Company.* Chicago: University of Chicago Press, 1950.

Faulkner, Harold U. *The Decline of Laissez–Faire, 1897–1917.* New York: Rinehart and Company, 1951.

Fiske, George Walter. *The Challenge of the Country: A Study of Country Life Opportunity.* New York: Young Men's Christian Association Press, 1912.

Fuller, Wayne. *RFD: The Changing Face of Rural America.* Bloomington: Indiana University Press, 1966.

Garland, Hamlin. *Main–Travelled Roads: Six Mississippi Valley Stories*. Boston: Arena Publishing Company, 1891.

The General Education Board: An Account of Its Activities, 1902–1914. New York: General Education Board, 1915.

Ghent, William J. *Our Benevolent Feudalism*. New York: The Macmillan Company, 1902.

Gill, Charles Otis, and Gifford Pinchot. *The Country Church: The Decline of Its Influence and the Remedy*. New York: The Macmillan Company, 1913.

Griswold, A. Whitney. *Farming and Democracy*. New York: Harcourt, Brace and Company, 1948.

Hagedorn, Hermann, ed. *The Works of Theodore Roosevelt*. National Edition. 20 volumes. New York: Charles Schribner's Sons, 1924–1926.

Harbaugh, William H. *The Life and Times of Theodore Roosevelt*. New Revised Edition. New York: Collier Books, 1963.

Hays, Samuel P. *Conservation and the Gospel of Efficiency; The Progressive Conservation Movement, 1890–1920*. Cambridge: Harvard University Press, 1959.

———. *The Response to Industrialism, 1885–1914*. Chicago: University of Chicago Press, 1957.

Hendrick, Burton J. *The Training of an American: The Earlier Life and Letters of Walter H. Page, 1855–1915*. Boston: Houghton Mifflin Company, 1928.

Hill, James J. *Highways of Progress*. New York: Doubleday, Page and Company, 1910.

Hofstadter, Richard. *The Age of Reform: From Bryan to F.D.R.* New York: Alfred A. Knopf, 1955.

Houston, David F. *Eight Years With Wilson's Cabinet, 1913 to 1921*. 2 volumes. Garden City, New York: Doubleday, Page and Company, 1926.

Kuznets, Simon. *National Income: A Summary of Findings*. New York: National Bureau of Economic Research, Inc., 1946.

Leornard, John W., and Albert N. Marquis, eds. *Who's Who in America: A Biographical Dictionary of Notable Living Men and Women of the United States*. I–XII. Chicago: A. N. Marquis Company, 1899–1922.

McConnell, Grant. *The Decline of Agrarian Democracy*. Berkeley: University of California Press, 1953.

McGeary, M. Nelson. *Gifford Pinchot, Forester–Politician*. Princeton: Princeton University Press, 1960.

Monroe, Paul, ed. *Cyclopedia of Education*. New York: The Macmillan Company, 1913.

Morison, Elting E., and John Blum, eds. *The Letters of Theodore Roosevelt*. 8 volumes. Cambridge: Harvard University Press, 1951–1954.

Mowry, George E. *The California Progressive*. Berkeley: University of California Press, 1951.

_____. *The Era of Theodore Roosevelt, 1900–1912.* New York: Harper and Brothers, 1958.

The National Cyclopedia of American Biography. New York: James T. White Company, 1891-1967.

Nourse, Edwin G. *The Legal Status of Agricultural Co-operation.* New York: The Macmillan Company, 1927.

Peffer, E. Louise. *The Closing of the Public Domain: Disposal and Reservation Policies, 1900–1950.* Stanford: Stanford University Press, 1951.

Pinchot, Gifford. *Breaking New Ground.* New York: Harcourt, Brace and Company, 1947.

_____. *The Fight for Conservation.* Garden City: Doubleday, Page and Company, 1911.

Plunkett, Sir Horace. *The Rural Life Problem of the United States. Notes of An Irish Observer.* New York: The Macmillan Company, 1910.

Robbins, Roy M. *Our Landed Heritage: The Public Domain, 1776– 1936.* Princeton: Princeton University Press, 1942.

Rodgers, Andrew Denny, III. *Liberty Hyde Bailey: A Story of American Plant Sciences.* Princeton: Princeton University Press, 1944.

Roosevelt, Theodore. *The Foes of Our Own Household. The Works of Theodore Roosevelt.* Edited by Hermann Hagedorn. Vol. XIX. New York: Charles Scribner's Sons, 1925.

Ross, Earle D. *Iowa Agriculture, An Historical Survey.* Iowa City: State Historical Society of Iowa, 1951.

Saloutos, Theodore, and John D. Hicks. *Agricultural Discontent in the Middle West, 1900–1939.* Madison: University of Wisconsin Press, 1951.

Shideler, James H. *Farm Crisis, 1919–1923.* Berkeley and Los Angeles: University of California Press, 1957.

Smith, Henry Nash. *Virgin Land: The American West as Symbol and Myth.* Cambridge: Harvard University Press, 1950.

Strong, Josiah. *Challenge of the City.* New York: Missionary Education Movement of the United States and Canada, 1911.

Sullivan, Mark. *Our Times: The United States, 1900–1925.* Volume III. New York: Charles Scribner's Sons, 1930.

Taeuber, Conrad, and Irene B. Taeuber. *The Changing Population of the United States.* Census Monograph Series. New York: John Wiley and Sons, 1958.

Taylor, H. C., and Anne Dewees Taylor. *The Story of Agricultural Economics in the United States, 1840–1932—Men, Services, Ideas.* Ames: Iowa State College Press, 1952.

Thompson, Warren S. *Population: A Study in Malthusianism.* New York: Columbia University Press, 1915.

Voorhies, Horace Jeremiah. *American Cooperatives: Where They Come From, What They Do, Where They Are Going.* New York: Harper and Brothers, 1961.

Wallace, Henry. *Uncle Henry's Own Story of His Life.* Volume III.

Des Moines: The Wallace Publishing Company, 1917.

Werner, M. R. *Julius Rosenwald: The Life of a Practical Humanitarian.* New York: Harper and Brothers, 1939.

Wilson, Warren H. *The Church of the Open Country: A Study of the Church for the Working Farmer.* New York: Missionary Education Movement of the United States and Canada, 1911.

————. *Quaker Hill: A Sociological Study.* New York: Columbia University Press, 1907.

The Works of Theodore Roosevelt. Executive Edition. 14 volumes. New York: P. F. Collier and Son, 1882-1903.

Index